Empower Yourself with Apple Shortcuts

The Intuitive Illustrated Guide for IOS Users

Empower Yourself with Apple Shortcuts

The Intuitive Illustrated Guide for IOS Users

Sumith Wanni Arachchige

ISBN: 9798329112146

To my lovely Lakdini.

To my mother, late father, my nephews, and Ahasna.

https://empoweryourselfwithappleshortcuts.tekcroach.top

Table of Contents

Preface

This book is on how to create Apple Shortcuts. This is not a compendium of Shortcuts either.

You are not expected to have any prior programming knowledge except a working knowledge of some Apple device, preferably an iPhone. You don't need to be an Apple expert to create or work with Shortcuts.

I do not consider Apple Shortcuts a very serious deep subject that requires you to dedicate your time and effort much. It is just a simple facility or feature; simple but useful.

Personally, I feel about Shortcuts in a different way – it's like a hobby to me. In my very simple life, I do not use Shortcuts much. Even the cutting-edge iPhone is just another cellular phone to me. But I always look for fascinating innovative features in devices – just for fun!

I think there are only a handful of books on Apple Shortcuts, and therefore I hope this book will receive a warm welcome by the Apple community.

I have written more than 18 books in both English and my mother tongue "Sinhala" (Sinhalese), but this book is rather different. Due to the nature of the subject matter, I decided to use a simple and illustrative style mostly.

```
I have used a distinctive font to render text
that you have to type in. This text is
written in that font.
```

In the same way, italic font is used to denote keywords, Action names, and things directly displayed on screens.

The actual Shortcuts screens on your device is colorful. They use different colors to signify different aspects. However, this book is presented in gray-scale (monochromatic) to lower the cost of the book, and therefore you will not see colorful exciting graphics in the book.

I wanted to make this book as small as possible. Who likes to read a thousand pages to learn a simple thing? I could have easily included hundreds of Shortcuts to show how to use every single Action available, but I did not. Anyway, I do encourage you to try them. It is really interesting.

Writing this book was a fun project for me, and I am extremely happy that I completed it just as I first planned it. Finally, I thank you for reading this book.

Sumith Wanni Arachchige

sumith@tekcroach.top

21st of Jun, 2024

Introduction

Now you have this book in your hand, I can assume you already possess an **iPhone** or an **iPad**, and know a thing or two about **Shortcuts**.

Therefore, I will directly walk you through the creation of a very simple Shortcut first. I think hands-on experience is much better than a lot of theories when it comes to learning this sort of things. Later we'll go into details step by step.

Create Your First Shortcut

When you create any Shortcut, you must open the Shortcuts app in your IOS device.

On my iPhone, I have put the Shortcut app on the first **Home Screen** like below.

Look for it in your Home Screen (the normal screen where you see your app icons), and still if you can't find it, you swipe left until you see the **App Library** screen where you can see all the apps installed on the device, if you will. There you enter Shortcut in the *search bar* and you will see it. Tap on it.

If you still couldn't find it, it may not have been installed on your device. Then you must install the Shortcuts app from within Apple **App Store**.

When you open the Shortcuts app, you will see the main screen like below on iPhone (the screen might look a bit different on iPad).

Sometimes you may see some shortcuts already setup there automatically for you. It's ok. All the Shortcuts you are going to create are stored in here. You can nicely organize, modify, and delete them.

In my iPhone, there are a few Shortcuts as you can see. Yours might look different.

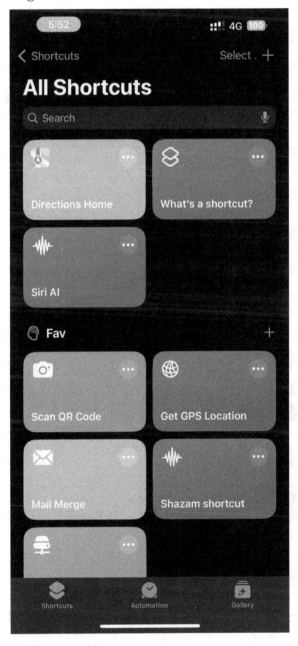

Ok. Now tap on the + sign at the top right corner.

That is how we create a new Shortcut. Then you will be presented with the following screen where you design and create your Shortcut. Always it is the same and only way to create a Shortcut – simple or complex.

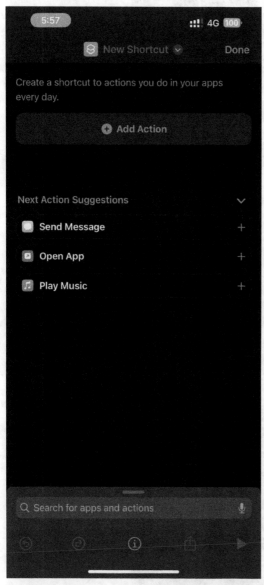

Read the screen and get familiarized with it. No haste indeed.

At the very top middle, you can see *New Shortcut*, and it is the automatically set name for our Shortcut we are going to create. You should always give a good short descriptive name for a Shortcut. For this trivial Shortcut, let's rename it to MyFirstShortcut. How to do that?

Tap on the name, and you will get a menu like shown. Tap on the *Rename* menu item. Then you type MyFirstShortcut or any other name you like for that matter. Finally tap on *Done* on the keypad. Done!

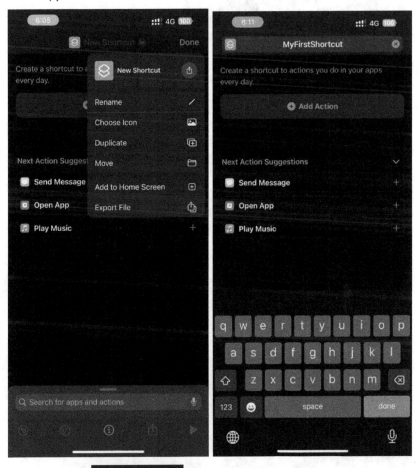

Now tap on ⊕ Add Action button. You'll get the following.

Actually, a *Shortcut* is a set of Actions. A Shortcut can have one or any number of Actions.

Actions are the capabilities of the Apple device (that is your iPhone or iPad).

The device offers us many interesting Actions. It is up to you to use those Actions in a meaningful way to get something useful and "magical".

In this trivial case, we are not going to experience the magic yet.

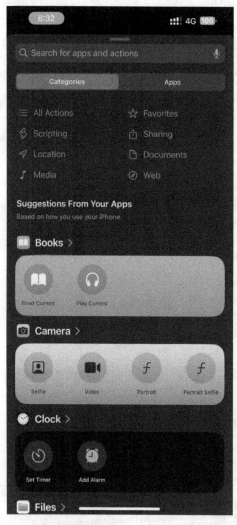

You can select the Action you want to include from this window. You have two ways to select an Action.

1. Tap on one of the categories – *All Actions, Favorites, Scripting, Location, Media, Sharing, Documents, Web.* Apple has categorized Actions like that for our convenience.

   As you can easily understand that *All Actions* category has all the Actions supported by the device. You will know about *Favorites* later.

2. You can search the Action by typing its name in the *Search bar.* As you keep typing in, the results will be getting narrowed down.

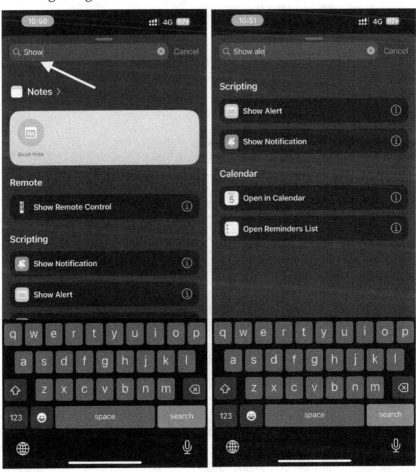

I think searching is the fastest way to select an Action, but you must remember the name of the Action for that. When the name of the Action that you want to include appears, tap on that.

I am going to use the Action *Show Alert*, and I can find it in Scripting. I tap on *Scripting*, and will be shown all the Actions under that category where I can scroll to find *Show Alert*.

If you do not know the category too (but you can surely guess it if you get familiar with Shortcuts), then tap on *All Actions* and scroll until you find the specific Action. So, select *Show Alert* from the list.

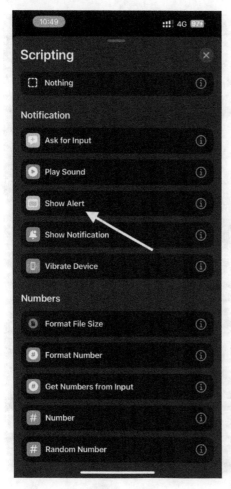

Now you will get back to the Shortcut creation window with the newly selected Action included (I have drawn a white box around it for more clarity).

The Action *Show Alert* does a very simple (yet very useful) task; that is to show something (some alert) on the screen. What is that "something"? It is some text.

You have to specify/write that text after the *Show Alert* statement. By default, that text is "*Do you want to continue?*". You should change it.

Just tap on the text. Then you can edit the text. In this example, let's completely delete it and write something else. I write "Greetings from Sumith for your first Apple Shortcut". Tap *Done*.

That's all. You just completed the first Shortcut creation.

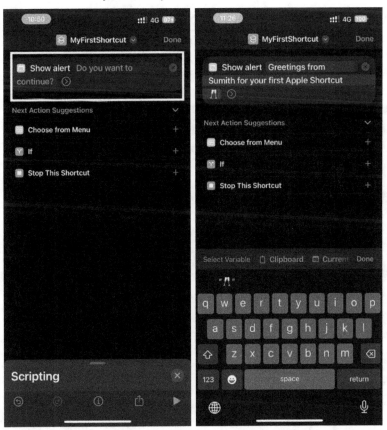

You can test it out now. Tap on the play button  at the bottom right of the window. It will run your newly created Shortcut. Our Shortcut is very small with just one Action. But it is a valid well-functioning Shortcut. It will show an alert like below.

You just press on either *Cancel* or *Ok* button, and the alert will disappear right away.

If you tap on Cancel in any alert or window, the Shortcut will stop right away!

Now tap on *Done* at the top right of the window to finish and get out of the Shortcut creation mode/window. That Shortcut is stored in your Shortcut app now. You will see under the *All Shortcuts* heading as shown here.

Tap on the Shortcut you just created, and it will run smoothly.

If a Shortcut stops working due to an error or whatever, don't worry.

An erratic Shortcut cannot harm your device. It just stops gracefully.

Now you have experienced how to create a simple Shortcut. Of course, creating a more complicated Shortcut needs further knowledge and "logical creativity". Let's go step by step.

Shortcuts and Actions

You have already tasted what Shortcut and Action are like. I think you can agree with me that they are not difficult to understand at all. Anyway, let's briefly have a formal understanding of them. You don't have to be a computer programmer or a highly analytical person to work with and create Shortcuts.

Shortcut is only a bundle of Actions. It could have only one Action or thousands of Actions (nevertheless, I have not created or not found a Shortcut with no more than a few dozens of Actions). You give a name to a Shortcut. You can delete it, modify it, share it, rename it at any time.

Actions inside a Shortcut are sequentially executed from the first/topmost Action to the last/bottommost Action. If any error occurs and a particular Action stops working, then the entire Shortcut stops at that point, and exits gracefully.

Action is a single operation or functionality provided by the device. A device has many such Actions at your disposal. You can consider a Shortcut as a chain of Actions as well. You insert Actions into a Shortcut such that the result of an Action is related to or fed as the input to the next Action – a chain.

Just have a peek at the available Actions for you to get an idea about what sort of functionalities are offered through Activities. You can see the list of Actions when you are modifying or creating a Shortcut. So, tap on + button in the Shortcuts main window (as if to create a new Shortcut). Then tap on *Add*

Action button again. Tap on *All Actions* to get the whole list of Actions available on your Apple device.

Actually, the Actions are organized alphabetically under several headings (like *Alarms, Calendar, Contacts, Documents, Folders, Health, Home, Location, Media, Scripting, Settings, Sharing, Stopwatch, Tabs, Text, Timer, Web, Workout*) for you to easily remember and find them.

You can easily understand the functionality of most Actions because their names are descriptive.

All the Actions are things that your device is capable of doing, and almost every day you too use the device to get those things done – set alarm, delete alarm, add an event to the calendar, edit or delete the even, text or call or email someone, add/edit/delete a contact, translate text, make a pdf, print a file, scan a QR, get your GPS coordinates (current location), play or pause a music, add or delete files, do some numeric calculations, and so on. Therefore, these Actions are not mysterious or unknown to you at all.

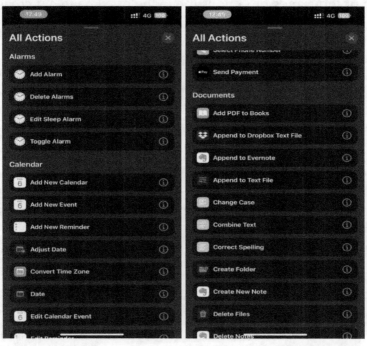

Not all Actions are alike.

Some Actions need some data (input) to work on. For example, the *Show Alert* Action we used in our trivial Shortcut needs some text to display in the alert. Remember?

Some Actions output data. For example, the Action *Get current IP address* does not require any input, but it outputs the current IP address that your device has obtained from the WiFi (if connected to a WiFi) or the mobile operator (if data connection is enabled).

Some Actions require both input and output.

Whenever you open the Shortcut app, you see the following three tabs at the bottom.

At the moment, just remember that we are working in the *Shortcuts* tab where all the Shortcuts on your device live in. Tap on *Shortcuts* to see your installed Shortcuts. We'll come to the other two tabs later.

Let's Create A Few Simple but Useful Shortcuts

These Shortcuts are simple, but not trivial. They are really useful. I know that you can handle your Apple device in a productive way. However, how productive you are with the phone depends on a number of factors.

First, you must learn and know how to operate the device in the correct optimum manner. You should have read the device manual well. You should know about what basic and advanced features your device supports.

Second, you must install the best apps to capitalize on the capabilities of the device.

Usually, I prefer to install free apps – free but not crippled. There are so many kind-hearted and capable people out there who have developed fantastic apps for free. (I am so grateful to them.)

Third, you must plan well and organize your work in such a way you can integrate the technology to make your life easier, more enjoyable, less stressful, and more productive.

In that journey, Shortcuts come in handy. Sometimes you can get things done quickly with Shortcuts, saving lots of clicks, swipes, and typing, and of course time as well.

Some Shortcuts enable you to do things that is, otherwise, impossible directly interacting with the device itself, without resorting to an external app utilizing that feature.

Our second Shortcut that we are going to create now gives us the current IP address of the device.

If you wanted to know the IP address currently assigned to your device, that functionality is limited in iPhone. If you are connected to a WiFi network, only then you can go to the WiFi settings on the device, and get it with several taps. But it is not so possible to get the IP when the device is using mobile data (3G, 4G, or 5G) from the mobile operator.

So, let's create a Shortcut to find the current IP address. Now I am not going to illustrate every obvious step to create a Shortcut because you have already seen them with illustrations in previous example.

Open the Shortcuts app, and automatically you are in the *Shortcuts* tab. If not, please tap on the *Shortcuts* tab.

Then tap on + to create a brand-new Shortcut.

Rename the Shortcut to something like `Get Current IP Address`.

Tap on *Add Action* to include the first Action.

Now you can either search or browse the Action. The Action you need to insert is *Get Current IP Address*. I prefer searching it by typing its name. Therefore, I type it and it appears when I partially typed `Get cu` in the search box. Tap on it.

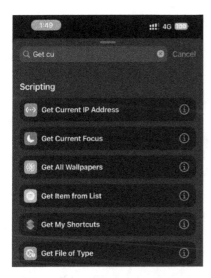

Now it is inserted. Test it out by tapping on the play button 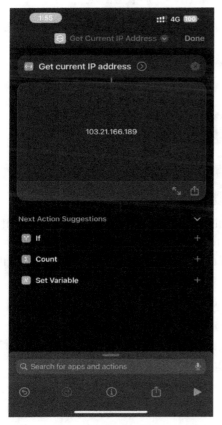.
You will see the result in the box just below the Action.

103.21.166.189

Now tap on *Done*, and your Shortcut is saved in the device.

Ok, let's run it now. Tap on the name of the Shortcut you just created.

Well, it did not show anything this time. What happened? Something went wrong? No, nothing went wrong. I'm pretty sure the Action still could obtain the IP address. But it is not shown/presented to you. Why? Because you did not insert an Action to present/show to you. We can use *Show Result* Action for that.

Modify a Shortcut

We now have to modify the Shortcut to insert another Action to it. The first Action retrieved the IP address. You must add *Show Result* Action to present the IP address so retrieved.

How to modify an existing Shortcut? Very simple. Tap on three dots on top right corner inside the Shortcut tile.

As you can see every Shortcut is shown as a tile (a rectangular shape). A **Shortcut tile** has a logo/symbol at its top left corner and its name at the bottom. You can even change the Shortcut symbol. We'll do that later.

To modify or edit an existing Shortcut, there is another way. **Long press** on the Shortcut (long press means keep pressing), and a menu appears. From that menu, tap on *Edit*, and you are taken to the Shortcut creation/modification screen.

You are now in the Shortcut modification screen, and you can see the Action in it. But there is no *Add Action* button visible. No worries. After the first Action added, you won't see it. Instead, you must insert new Actions from the box as shown in the below picture.

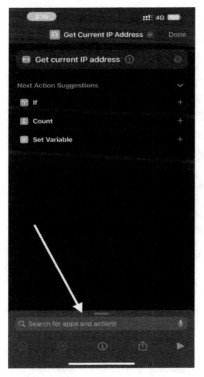

Tap on this *Search for apps and actions* box, and you will immediately see the usual Actions list.

Search our second Action *Show Result* and tap on it. Now it will be added as the next Action inside the Shortcut.

A wonderful thing has really happened here. Can you notice it? Carefully look what is written after Show. It's *Current IP Address.*

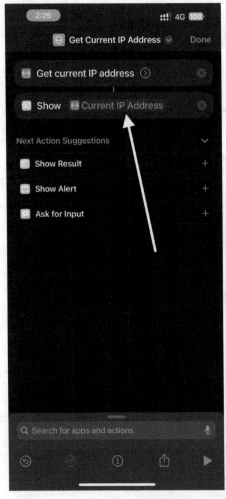

Current IP Address is not just some text (ie, a literal) as you saw in *Show Alert* Action. This is called a **variable**. We often use a lot of variables in our Shortcuts. We'll investigate variables in a moment. Don't worry.

Now tap on the play button to test it. Or you can tap on *Done*, and then tap on the Shortcut to run it. You will now see the IP address. Tap on either *Done* or *Cancel* button to dismiss it.

Is this really your public IP address? You can google `what is my IP?`, and the google will tell your IP address. Compare this with the Google result. The second Shortcut was successfully created.

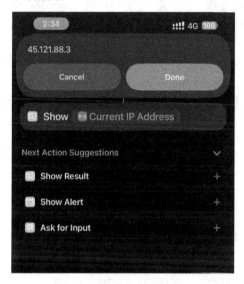

Variable

Those who have learned computer programming know what variables are and how crucial and indispensable they are. Don't worry if you haven't done programming because I will explain it very simply. No computer programming knowledge is needed for Shortcuts.

A variable is a storage for some data.

That data might be a number like *47, 294850672830, 405.742*; or a string like *Sumith, Sri Lanka*; or an image or a video or some other data. The variable is just a storage or a placeholder for that data.

A variable has a name or identifier (id) to refer to it. Here, "refer to" means to write/store some data at that space (memory space/location) or to read the data stored/written in that memory location. That's it.

In the above example, *Current IP Address* is a variable. In Apple Shortcuts, a variable name can have spaces in-between (in computer programming variable names cannot have spaces)

Why do we use variables? Actually, we will not be able to create any productive Shortcuts if we did not have variables. Often, we want some data item again and again in several Actions. We could save that data item in a variable, and use that variable (by its name) again and again later. Or sometimes we do not want to use the output of some Action in the immediately following Action, but instead we want to use it in later Actions. Here too, we store that output of that Action in a variable so you can refer to it later.

In Apple Shortcuts, you find basically two kinds of variables.

1. Magic variables
2. User-defined (explicit) variables.

Magic variables are not created by you; they are automatically generated out of the operation of Actions in the Shortcut.

I told you earlier that an Actions can output some data. Actually, Apple Shortcut system (ecosystem) always creates a separate variable for the output of an Action. These are called magic variables.

In the above example, Apple ecosystem automatically creates for you a magic variable called *Current IP Address*.

Apple often chooses a good descriptive name for magic variables, depending on the context. In our example, we used the Action *Get Current IP Address*. So, obviously the output of that Action is the current IP address of your device, hence the variable name *Current IP Address*. You too must name your explicit user-defined variables in meaningful descriptive way.

Improving the Get Current IP Address Action

The above Action retrieves and shows on the screen the current IP address of the device. What if you want to copy it? You can of course remember it by heart and then type it in somewhere else. But it's lame. Isn't it? Let's enhance our Shortcut to automatically copy that IP address.

Whatever you copy in your device is temporarily stored in what is called the **clipboard**. It can store very small or very big data items; you don't have to worry about the size of the data item you copy.

So, we are now going to copy the retrieved IP address in the clipboard. For that you need to use another Action called *Copy to Clipboard*. Insert it. You now know how to insert an Action.

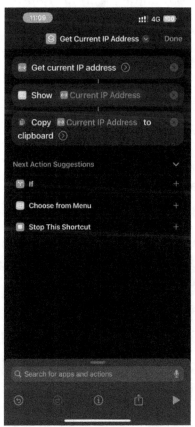

Well, for one more time, I will guide you in case you don't remember it – the last time. Go to the Shortcuts app, and tap on the three dots on the *Get Current IP Address* Shortcut you just created. Type in *Copy to Clipboard* in the search box at the bottom of the window, and tap on it. That's it.

New Actions are added to the end of the Actions list. Now when you run this Shortcut, first it runs the topmost Action to retrieve your current IP address, then executes the second Action to present that IP address on screen, and executes the last Action you just added to copy that same IP address. Pretty simple!

I prefer to change the order of our Actions; I want to bring the copy Action just before the show Action. How to do it? You long press on the copy Action, and then drag carefully above the show Action. Or else you can long press on the show Action and drag it down. Either will do it.

Remember not to press just on the variable name. You can long press on the Action symbol or an empty space inside the Action rectangle. If you long pressed correctly, you will see that rectangle swells a bit to notify you it is ready to be dragged now.

Even if you could drag Actions up or down as you wish, you must be careful with it. In this particular example, it does not matter whether the show Action is above or below the copy Action. However, you cannot drag the copy or show Action above the Get Current IP Address Action. Why? It's not a logical order. First get the current IP address, then copy it – that's the logical order. Right? Exercise your common sense!

Again, I want you to notice something that we learnt a while ago – about magic variables. In this example, both the copy and the show actions use the same magic variable that was generated from the first Action. I told you that we use a variable again and again.

Modifying Variables and Properties of Action

It's time to learn a couple of things here. Look at the Shortcut again. See the sections I have pointed at with arrows.

What are those tiny vertical bars that I have shown with arrows numbered 1? Such a vertical bar shows us that the two Actions above and below it are related to each other. That means the below Action is fed the output of the above Action.

Wait a second. I said the bar relates the two Actions immediately above and below it. But the magic variable *Current IP Address* is the output of the first Action. Right? Well, that is correct. The *Copy to Clipboard* Action does not output anything; it just copies to the clipboard. However, the show

Action still gets the same data item the copy Action got. So, the Apple ecosystem recognizes it as a continuous relation.

Let's check if it is so (as I described in the previous paragraph). Tap on the variable of the show Action (ie, tap on the *Current IP Address* part in front of *Show*), and you will see something like below (left image).

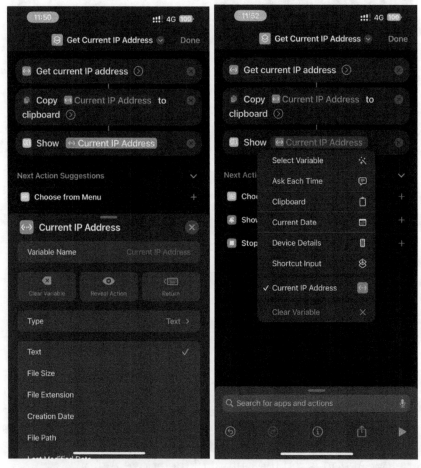

Tap on *Clear Variable* button, and the variable of the Show Action gets deleted. Don't just focus on other options you see there in the menu for now.

You can also delete a variable by long pressing on the variable name, and tapping on the *Clear Variable* menu item from the pop-up menu (top right image).

Now you will see Result (lightly dimmed) in front of Show. Such a dimmed text means nothing is there. Just test it out by pressing on the play button. It does not show any useful information.

Well, you write your name or anything for that matter in there; tap on the dimmed Result, and type in. Test it again, and now you see what you typed in there; not useful again. Right?

After you deleted the *Current IP Address* variable, you could not see the vertical bar too. That means the *Show Result* Action is not related to the Actions above it – it functions independently.

Ok, now let's put it in order. How to set a variable? Very easy. Long press on the variable, and you will again get the pop-up menu you saw a moment ago (top right image). You will see the list of available variables in that list. Select *Current IP Address* from the list, and that's it. The vertical bar appears again. I'll put that pop-up menu below.

What about the other options (menu items) in this menu? You know about *Clear Variable* and *Current IP Address. Clipboard, Current Date, Device Details, Shortcut Input* are also magic variables (anyway, the official Apple documentation call them **special variables**).

I told you that output of an Action is automatically stored in a separate magic variable. That is how the Current IP Address cropped up in that menu. Moreover, the Apple ecosystem also creates a few more magic variables for us to use. They are always created regardless of your Actions; they are global.

Device Details is one such global magic variable. It gives you means to retrieve some important details about your device (like Device Model, Screen Height, Screen Width, System Version, OS, Current Brightness, Current Volume, Name, etc.).

Current Date is another global magic variable. It gives you the current date and time on the device. You can do many operations with it.

Now you can guess what *Clipboard* is. It gives access to the clipboard of your device. When you copy anything in the device, that data is stored temporarily in the clipboard. When you copy another data item, the old data item stored in the clipboard is overwritten.

When you select *Ask Each Time*, you are prompted to enter some input when the Action runs. It may be handy for some Actions where the user interaction is necessary.

Shortcut Input is one of the most important magic variables. You can understand how the output of an Action can be stored in a magic variable, and how the global magic variables we just discussed come into play.

Actually, when you run a Shortcut, you can input some data into the Shortcut itself. This data item is not generated within the Shortcut, but rather is fed into it when it starts running. If such data item exists, that data item can be accessed with this *Shortcut Input* variable. We'll do many examples using all of these global magic variables later.

Finally, let's see what *Select Variable* means. It lets you select a magic variable <u>visually</u>. This menu item is only shown if you have several Actions in the Shortcut (if the Shortcut has only one Action, you cannot see this). Tap on *Select Variable*, and you will see the following screen.

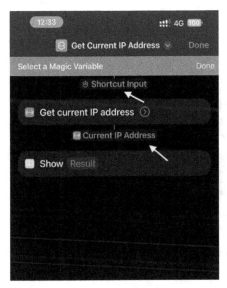

It shows you the available variables for you to use in the Action. I have drawn arrows to clearly show you what those variables are in our example. For the *Show Result* Action, we could select one of the two – *Shortcut Input* or *Current IP Address*.

Just tap on the variable you want to use. In our example, the *Current IP Address* is the one we need. Tap on it, and that variable is automatically populated in the box. Very easy.

Most Actions also have additional **Action properties** associated with it.

Let's take the *Get Current IP Address* Action for example. Your device might have an IPv4 address, or an IPv6 address, or even the both. On the other, if your device is connected to a local network, it might be assigned two IP address – one local IP address (mostly starting like 10.x.x.x or 172.x.x.x or 192.168.x.x) and one global IP address. So, you must specify these details if you execute the *Get Current IP Address* Action. How do you set these additional properties?

Refer to the first image at the beginning of this heading. See the arrow numbered 2? Tap on the little arrow symbol ⊘ beside the Action name. The properties panel will expand under the Action name now. You can see the two properties of this Action. Tap on the property value to select the appropriate setting. You must have a knowledge of the pertinent technical aspect to select the correct setting (in this case, you must know about IP addresses)

If you investigate the *Show Result* Action, you won't find any property associated with it. Thus, some Actions don't have properties. Most of the time, the Apple ecosystem will select the default (mostly used) settings for you; but you can change them anytime and you should indeed.

Create Shortcuts

Now that you have a working understanding of Shortcuts, we should focus more on the design aspects rather than the technical aspect of Shortcut creation.

You should be familiarized with the user interface of the Shortcuts App, the basic terminology and concepts, and a rough understanding of the Actions available on your device. Again, I kindly invite you to go through each and every Action.

When I browsed the list now, I stumbled upon the following section (left bottom) and I was interested to know more about the *Get Current Location* Action. Tap on the ⓘ symbol to get a description about that particular Action (right bottom).

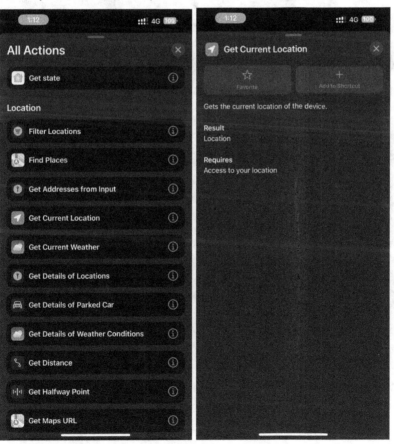

As you can see it has a brief description of the Action. It tells you the prerequisites for this Action to run. For this particular Action, it needs access to the Location privilege on your device. That means you must first enable Location service on your device.

For that, open the **Settings** app (steps to be followed on an iPhone), then go to *Privacy & Security*, and tap on *Location Services*, and again tap on the toggle switch/button in front of the *Location Services*.

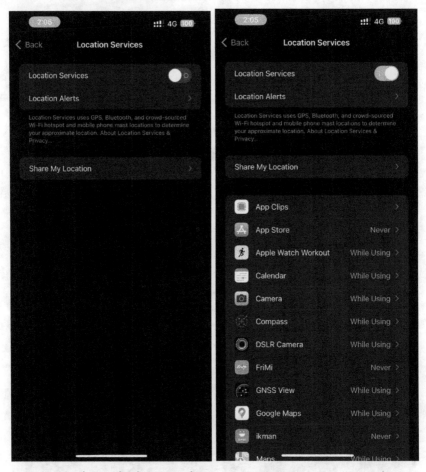

Most people including me keep Location Services (in other words the GPS) turned off for several reasons. This service drains the battery much. On the other, it is kind of letting you be tracked real-time. I only enable it when I need some location/GPS based function.

The description panel also gives you an idea about the output of the Action. In this case, it says the output or the result is a Location object.

Object can be considered as a generic term to refer to any data type. So, an object might be a simple text, a number, a formatted text, a formatted number, and so on.

What did I mean by "formatted" above? Formatting is making a string or a number according to a pattern.

Take for example an email address. Email address is not just a text; it has some structure in it.

> There is some alphanumeric part at the front and an @ followed by some other alphanumeric part, and a dot followed by a few characters, like sumith@tekcroach.top.

Date is another good example for a formatted data item. It has to be written like 4-21-2024 or 21-Apr-24 and so on.

Get Your Current GPS Location

First of all, let me tell you that the GPS (Global Positioning System) is almost synonymous with the latitude, longitude points of a position on the Earth.

Actually, GPS is just the pioneering service provided by the US; and Galileo by Europe, GLONAS from Russia, Beidou from China are some other such services. All of these services are collectively known as Global Navigation Satellite System (GNSS).

Modern devices are capable of using all of these satellite systems to determine the location.

Not only that, the device can even utilize (some) WiFi networks to determine the location. You do not have to be an expert in these nitty gritty to use Location services, though.

Let's create a Shortcut to get the current Location, then copy the latitude and longitude pair, and then to show them on the screen.

Open the Shortcuts App.

Create a new Shortcut tapping on +.

Rename the Shortcut to `Get My Current Location` (or something meaningful to you).

Tap on *Add Action*, and search *Get Current Location*, and tap on it. You will see something like following left.

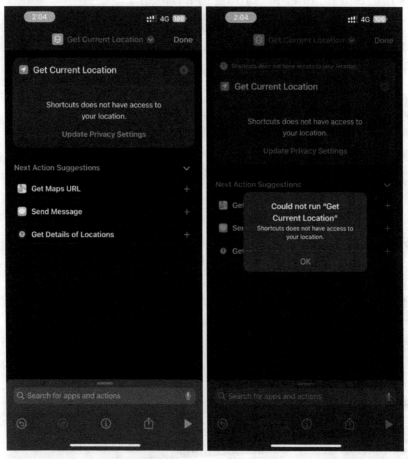

Just below the *Get Current Location* Action, you can see a message saying "*Shortcuts does not have access to your location.*" It simply means that you have disabled Location

Services on your device. Without doing anything else, just test it out, and you will see an error message as in the top right image.

Enable it (I showed you how to do it a moment ago). If you had already enabled it on your device, you won't see this error message.

Now test the Shortcut to get your current location as follows.

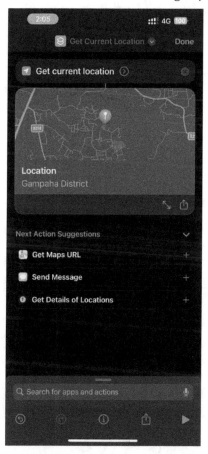

It works, but it is not so useful still. Let's copy the latitude and longitude separated by a comma (with no spacing).

Insert *Copy to Clipboard* Action.

The magic variable *Current Location* is automatically filled in for you. Why Current Location? Well, the Apple ecosystem is smart enough to guess it based on the context. The previous Action was to retrieve a Location object (that is, your current location), and it thinks that you want to copy it to the clipboard. If it not what you want, of course you can change it, but it is really what you want to do here.

Now let's show the same location on screen. We can use the *Show Result* Action for that. Insert it, and *Current Location* is already populated in there.

That's it. Test it out. You get something like this.

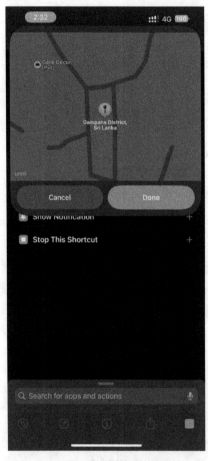

We expected GPS coordinates (ie, longitude, latitude, altitude), but we have received a visual location. How to get the numerical values from this Action. Very easy. But before that, I want to discuss another important matter here.

The *Get Current Location* Action outputs a Location object. See its details if you like (we have learnt how see the details of an Action).

There is another way to see the details of an Action. Tap on the small icon at the beginning of an Action name, and you will get a pop-up menu. Tap on *Show Info* in that list, you are shown the details of that Action.

Don't tap on *Remove*, it will delete your Action right away. You can also delete an Action just by tapping on ⊗ beside the Action name.

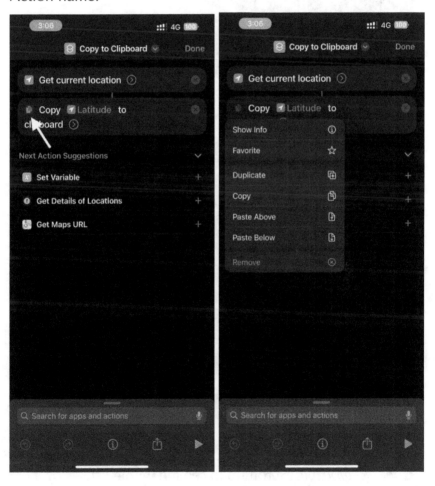

The Location object has many data items in it, and longitude and latitude are two such data items integrated in a Location object.

You can see all the individual data items in a Location object by tapping on a Location object. In our example, you can tap on *Current Location* variable (this variable holds a Location object as you now know).

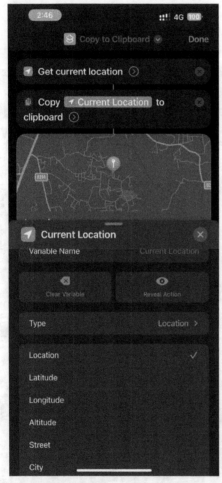

As you can see in the picture, there is a whole list of items – *Location, Latitude, Longitude, Altitude, Street, City, State, ZIP Code, Region*, etc. Scroll up to see the whole list.

We can tell an Action not to present/output the whole Location object as it is, but to present only a single data item in it.

This is how we achieve it. Tap on the Location variable which is *Current Location*. Then tap on the required data item in that list. Let's tap on *Latitude*, and tap on the x to dismiss the menu.

Now you can see *Latitude* after *Copy*. That means instead of the whole Location object, we are just copying the latitude.

Test it, and you will get something as follows. Now we've got a numerical value (I struck out some part to hide my location). It works!

If you had selected *Longitude* instead of *Latitude*, you would have got the longitude. But we want to retrieve the both, separated by a comma. How to get it? With the copy Action you can't directly do it. We can employ a trick to get it done. Yeah, we often have tricks!

My thinking is like this.

> I first construct a formatted text; that is, I want to have a formatted text like "**longitude,latitude**". This text is then input to the copy Action.

This trick is very handy, so keep it in mind. We construct the formatted text in a Text Action, and then feed it into the next Action!

To construct this formatted text, I use another Action named *Text*. Insert it into the Shortcut, and drag it just above the copy Action.

You can write anything in this *Text*. You can write strings/text, numbers, punctuation marks, or whatever. You can even include variables inside this text. You can mix them together too. That is the real power of *Text*.

Now we are going to first include the latitude variable, then a comma, and then the longitude variable in this *Text*. Let's do it.

Tap in the input box just below the *Text* Action name. You can write anything here. But we don't want to write anything other than the latitude, then a comma, lastly the longitude.

Look at the strip I have shown with an arrow. In this strip, you can see the whole list of variables available to be used. Scroll left and right to find the variable *Current Location*, and tap on it.

The variable is inserted into the *Text*, and another panel opens for you to select an individual data item in the Location object.

Tap on *Latitude*, and the variable name inside Text changes accordingly.

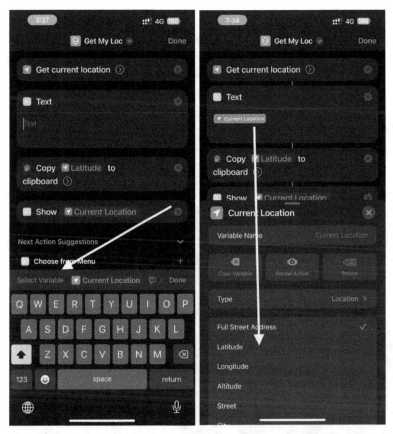

We are not over yet; we have to insert a comma now. Can you see a little keyboard symbol with **Return** underneath it? Tap on it to let us write or include more in the Text. Now you are back to the keyboard.

If you press the delete key on the keyboard, it will delete the inserted variable. It's ok; do it. Nobody is going to punish you. Now again add it back by selecting *Current Location* from the strip, and changing it to a Latitude variable as was done previously.

After you added the *Latitude*, tap on the *Return*, and then type in a comma.

Then we must include the *Longitude* variable. Do the same. You can still see the *Select Variable* strip just above the keyboard. Select *Current Location* from it, and change it to *Longitude*. Then press on x to dismiss the panel.

We have completed constructing/formatting the text.

Now we have to ask the copy Action to copy it. Long press on the variable name beside the Copy (in my case, it is populated with the Latitude variable which is not what I wanted). Select *Text* from the list. *Text* variable was magically created by inserting the *Text* Action (remember magic variables we discussed before?)

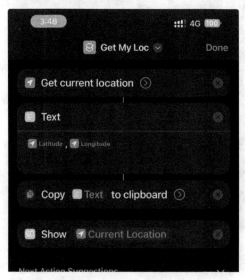

Now carefully read your Shortcut. The first Action retrieves your Location details from your GPS sensor in the device. Then we constructed a formatted text using *Text* Action. We included in the text two variables extracted from the result of the *Get current location* Action. Then the copy Action copies this *Text* into clipboard.

How do you want the last result, though? Do you want it to be shown on a map as before, or do you just want the numerical values of latitude and longitude?

If you wanted it to be shown on a map, leave *Current Location* as the variable of *Show*.

If you just want to get the numerical values of the coordinates, then leave *Text* as its variable. You try the both.

We constructed a very useful Shortcut. How do you know if the copied data is correct? Run the Shortcut, and open any text window that allows you to type in (email, sms, Note, Whatsapp or whatever), and paste. You can see that your longitude and latitude pair is nicely pasted. It works!

With this example, you learned how to extract individual data items from a compound object. Date object also has many data items that you can extract as you wish. You can now experiment with different data items inside an object. Nothing to worry; use your general knowledge.

QR and Barcode Scan Shortcut

QR codes and bar codes have become indispensable in the society now.

A QR is just some text, and that text might be a web URL, an email, a telephone, a code, or any string for that matter.

A barcode is simply a number string.

However, it is not able to carry much data in both of them.

Your iPhone's native camera app is able to scan QR codes, but it can't scan barcodes; I don't know why. However, you do not need another third-party app to scan barcodes. Apple device inherently has that capability too. Let's create a Shortcut to scan both QR and Barcode.

Open the Shortcuts app, and make sure you are in the *Shortcuts* tab.

Press on + to create a new Shortcut.

Rename the Shortcut to `Scan Code` or to something meaningful to you.

Tap on *Add Action*, and search and select *Scan QR or Barcode*.

This Action will open your camera and let you scan a QR or Barcode. It is a very simple but so useful Action. It has no properties to set. It takes no input, but outputs a Barcode object.

Now get a barcode or a QR code around you and scan it with the Shortcut. It will show what is encoded in the code. Success!

Let's improve it now. We'll save the URL into the clipboard and show it on the screen. You know how to do it. Right?

Insert the Action *Copy to Clipboard,* and the QR/Barcode variable is automatically set for you. Well done, Apple!

Insert the Action *Show Result* too.

That's it. Tap on Done to dismiss the window. Run the Shortcut and scan your codes now.

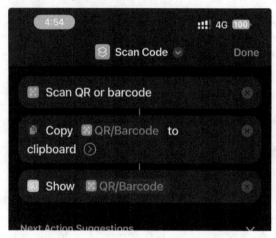

Gallery

At the bottom right of the Shortcuts app you have *Gallery.* Gallery is the place you can find lots of Shortcuts created by others. You can import Shortcuts from there. Remember that not all the Shortcuts there are good. Just tap on a Shortcut that looks interesting to you and you will see a description of it like below.

You can import/import this Shortcut into your (private) collection by tapping on *Add Shortcut.* Or you can view inside the Shortcut without importing it, by tapping on the three dots on the Shortcut tile shown in the middle. Tap on *Cancel* to dismiss it without importing.

You can also import a Shortcut by clicking on the + sign at the top right corner of a Shortcut tile in the Gallery. If a particular Shortcut is already added, the + is replaced with a check/right sign. Play with some Shortcuts on the Gallery to get some insight about Shortcuts.

Show Directions from Current Location Shortcut

It's really very convenient to get directions from your current location to some other destination. We mainly use either the Google Map or the Apple Map for that. Let's create a Shortcut to get directions from either map app.

Open the Shortcuts app, and make sure to land on the *Shortcuts* tab.

Tap on + to create the Shortcut, and rename it to Get Directions.

Add the *Get Directions* Activity.

It requires several details/properties/parameters to function.

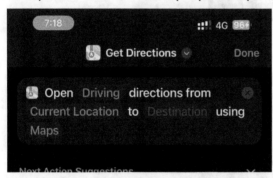

Tap on *Driving* and you will see a list of mode of traveling – *Driving, Walking, Biking*. Select an appropriate mode for you. If you mostly walk, then select *walking*.

You can set the starting location by tapping on the *Current Location* (the field just after "*directions from*"). It's better leave it with the *Current Location*. Then the map app gives directions from where you are now.

Then you must set the destination by tapping on the field next to "*to*". Enter a destination here.

If you set a destination preset like this, this Shortcut always will show the directions to that destination from the current location.

You can long press on it, and select *Ask Each Time* too. Then, the Shortcut prompts you to type in a location when it is run.

Finally, you can set the map app you are going to use with this Shortcut to give you the directions. Tap on the field just after "*using*" and you will see *Maps* and *Google Maps* in the list. Select your preferred map app (I prefer Google map).

Or you can set the map field to *Ask Each Time* too. Then, you are prompted to choose your map app at the run time. If you select this option, the mode of travel field is discarded from the Action, and you will have to select the mode of travel too at the run time.

Speak Out Shortcut

With the **Text-to-Speech (TTS)** technology, any text can be easily read out (spoken) now. Depending on the TTS engine used in the device, the spoken content may be kind of robotic or as natural as a real human speaking.

Let's create a Shortcut to read out a text. This Shortcut is going to fun in the end.

Create a new Shortcut and rename it to `Speak Out`.

Insert the first Action *Make Spoken Audio from Text*.

Tap on the *Text* field and enter some text (something like `Hi there`).

Test it now. You will hear the text you entered. It's still not useful enough though.

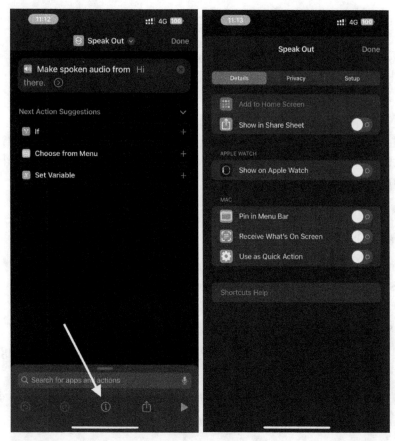

You can customize it to your needs. Well, for starters I want it to read out any web page I am browsing/reading in Safari. Therefore, I want to instruct my Shortcut to get the text from a web page in Safari. This is actually a brand-new functionality that we are going to explore.

Tap on the ⓘ at the bottom of the window. You will see another panel as shown in above right picture. It has three tabs – *Details*, *Privacy*, and *Setup*. In this project, we work in the *Details* tab only. What are those settings or options?

What is important to us are the options of *Show in Share Sheet*, and *Receive What's On Screen*. Toggle on (enable) the *Show in Share Sheet option* now. Tap on *Done*.

You are back in the Shortcut editor window. You can see that another block (I have marked it with a rectangle) has been added at the beginning as in the following left image.

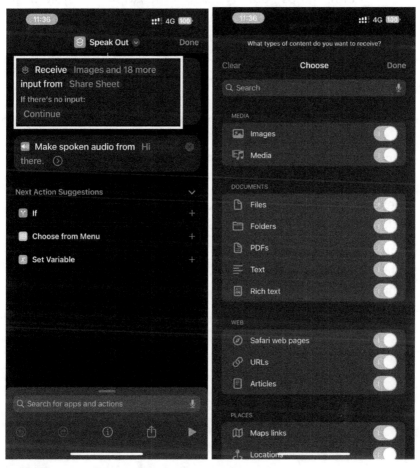

You have to tweak it further. Tap on *Images and 18 more* field just after *Receive*. It will open a new panel with a lot of toggle buttons as shown in the above right picture.

All the toggle buttons (18 of them) are automatically enabled (toggled on). But it's not a good practice to enable them all like that. What do they do indeed?

Apple device can save many different types of data – audio files in many different formats, video files in many different formats, different types of text files, PDF, web pages, email addresses, telephone numbers (because iPhone is primarily dealing with phone numbers), Location objects, map links, and so on.

This panel lists those data types that the Apple ecosystem supports. This panel allows you to instruct the device to associate or bind your Shortcut with those data types. If you enable all of those types, it means your Shortcut is forced to work on all of those types (and files).

But think for a moment. Does this Shortcut work with all of them? This Shortcut is going to read text. Then audio or video file type (media), map links, iTunes products, App Store apps, Contacts, Images, URL, Email addresses, Phone numbers are not compatible with this Shortcut.

Therefore, you should switch them off. Keep PDFs, Text, Rich text, Safari web pages, Articles toggled on.

I think you it is not difficult for you to understand what these data types mean and how they should be handled. They are simple and obvious.

After setting those association settings, tap on the field just after the *input from*. We have met this settings page before. Remember we selected *Show in Share Sheet*? That setting is already done.

Tap on the *Continue* field and a pop-up menu appears.

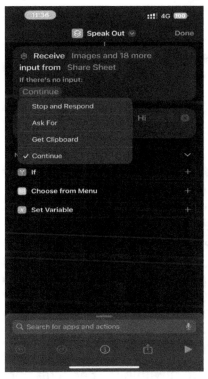

There are four options there. These options determine what the Shortcut should do in case the Shortcut did not get any appropriate input (ie, text) to work with. For example, the text may not be English or may not be in a recognized language.

Stop and Respond option means the Shortcut is stopped. If you selected it, you have to type in the response (error message) that is shown on the screen before quitting.

Ask for option means to prompt you type in some text and read it.

Get Clipboard option instructs the Shortcut to get whatever text saved in the clipboard (but we don't know whether the clipboard has some text at that moment, and even if it had text, that text might be some garbage). But we can use it deliberately if we first place the text in clipboard before running the Shortcut.

The *Continue* option means just to ignore the error, and execute the next Action.

You think about the scenarios when you can use the appropriate options for your Shortcut. In our example, select the *Stop and Respond* option, type in `oops! mayday mayday mayday`.

You must change the variable in the *Make Spoken Audio* Action now. Change it to *Shortcut Input.*

Magic Variable Shortcut Input

This is the first time we are going to use this magic variable. *Shortcut Input* variable holds the data that is input to the Shortcut when the Shortcut starts. This data comes from outside. Actually, this is the input text coming from an external text file or web page that is to be spoken out.

In this example, we are going to run this Shortcut on a web page in Safari. It means you will run this Shortcut from within Safari (I'll show you how to run it in a moment).

You are not supposed to run it from within the Shortcuts app like we have been doing in our previous examples. If you do it, the Shortcut immediately stops and responds with *"oops! mayday mayday mayday"*. Why so? Because that is how we instructed to behave because we want this Shortcut reads a webpage.

The web page on which the Shortcut is run will be the content/input to this Shortcut. So, web content is temporarily saved in the magic variable *Shortcut Input,* and the Actions in the Shortcut has now access to that content from within the Shortcut through that magic variable. Genius!

Ok, we have set all right. Tap on *Done* to finish the Shortcut creation. Run the Shortcut in the usual way by clicking on it from within the Shortcuts app (surely going to crash, but do it anyway). You will see the error message. Right? It does not work like that. Then, how does it work?

Open Safari web browser, and go to any website (better if the web page has some English content/text; it obviously can't read pictures, sounds, videos, animations, or any non-textual content).

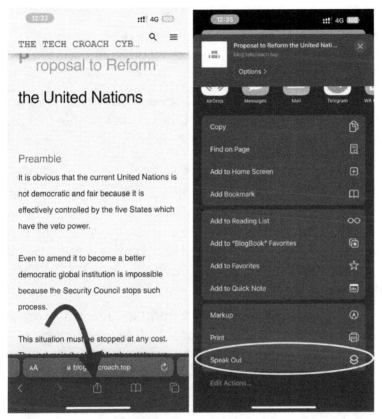

Now tap on the **Share button** (as shown in the above left picture) to get the share panel as shown in the above right picture. There you can see our *Speak Out* Shortcut.

When you enable *Show in Share Sheet* option for our Shortcut, this is what happens – the Shortcut is inserted into the share panel.

But this *Speak Out* Shortcut won't be shown if you try it on a video or audio or image file because we switched off those data types as we cannot read out those files.

Now everything makes sense. Doesn't it? Try opening an image, and tap on the share button, but you won't see the Shortcut.

Ok. Now open that web page again, tap on the share button, and tap on *Speak Out*. It will read out the web page. Oh no! No sound comes out. What's wrong? There is a problem still.

Make Spoken Audio from Action actually does not speak out. It just creates the audio out of the text. Another Action is needed to produce the sound.

Insert the *Quick Look* Action. *Quick Look* is a versatile Action, it does our job well too. *Spoken Audio* is the variable that holds the created audio by the previous Action.

Now test the Shortcut again. It works. Fantastic!

You can further tweak the TTS engine. Explore the properties in the *Make Spoken Audio From* Action. You can change the rate of speech, the pitch of the speck, and even the language. Apple TTS supports several languages besides English – Arabic, Chinese, French, Japanese, Hindi, German, Russian, Spanish, and so on.

> Unfortunately, it does not support my magical mother tongue (Sinhalese) yet. In case you like to learn Sinhalese, I have published a book on Amazon (*Learn Spoken Sinhala The Most Unconventional Sinhala Learner's Guide*).

You can also change the Voice of the TTS. There are several male and female voices to choose from. Experiment with the TTS settings to select a pleasing sound.

Create Shortcuts with Power

You have learned the basics of Shortcuts and also created a few useful Shortcuts. However, there are a few advanced "tools" or rather "constructs" hidden inside Shortcuts that you can use to create more advanced ones.

In this chapter, we are going to talk about execution of Actions in conditional and repeating fashion; if you are already familiar with programming, I know you got what I just mentioned, but for those who are not so, be patient and you will master it within the next few moments.

In programming, **commands/statements/instructions** are executed one after another. You saw it in Shortcuts too – Actions were executed one after another (the first Actions runs, then the second Action runs, then runs the third Action, and so on until the last Action runs and the Shortcut ends). This is called sequential execution or just a sequence.

You find three ways of execution of instructions/statements/commands in programming or in Actions of Shortcuts.

1. Sequence
2. Conditional (or Jump or Selection)
3. Repetition (or Loop)

As you probably can understand now, Shortcut creation is also kind of programming, but is much much simpler than programming proper. If you have already some programming experience, Shortcuts will be just a breeze for you. But if you don't know anything about programming, still you are just as fine because you are going to learn all the important things with this book.

What is Conditional?

Conditional is the execution of different sets of Actions (or statements as in general programming) based on some condition. Consider the following scenario for instance.

Mom: Would you like coffee or tea?

You: Tea please.
       I'd like some biscuits too.
       Add more sugar to the tea.

Or you could have responded as follows also.

Mom: Would you like coffee or tea?

You: Coffee please.
       No sugar.

Look carefully. This is a conditional. Your response was conditional. Isn't it? It could be either Tea or Coffee. If it were Coffee, your subsequent expressions may be different than if you had wanted Tea.

In your day-to-day life, you come across a number of such "conditional" situations where you have to make a choice out of a set of possible alternatives. That's why conditional is also known as **selection**.

But, why is it called **jumping**? Look at the following image and you will understand it. The execution depends on the choice, and it jumps to the relevant section accordingly.

Mom: Would you like coffee or tea? IF Coffee

You: Tea please.   IF Tea
       I'd like some biscuits too.
       Add more sugar to the tea.

You: Coffee please.
       No sugar.

Naturally, you tend to think or say something like **If this, then do this; or else do that**. Therefore, a conditional is informally known as an **IF statement/construct** as well.

Not so surprisingly now, Shortcuts offers *IF* Action for us to do conditional execution of Actions which we will be exploring in a moment.

What is repetition?

As the term itself implies, it means to repeat one or a set of Actions. It can repeat in two ways.

1. It can repeat a fixed number of times. For example, flip the pages of a book 7 times (so, you would have flipped only seven pages regardless of the number of pages of the book).

2. It can repeat any number of times as long as some condition is satisfied. For example, flip the pages of a book until all the pages are all flipped. Here the number of repetitions depends on the number of the pages in the book.

Apple Shortcuts offers two Repeat Actions – *Repeat,* and *Repeat with Each,* to achieve the both types of repetition.

Now let's create a few Shortcuts using the conditional and repetition constructs. The first few Shortcuts we are going to create will be trivial but they will clearly teach you how to use these constructs.

Trivial If

The first Shortcut is going to greet you either Good Morning or Good Evening depending on the time of the day. The expression itself hints that you need an IF construct to execute it. How? It includes "depending on", and that is conditional!

Open the Shortcuts app, and create a new Shortcut named IF Trivia.

Insert the *If* construct (Action). Type `if` and you'll find it.

After you added it, you can see something like above; it has inserted three parts – *If, Otherwise, End If. If* always comes with these three parts, but only *If* and *End If* parts are mandatory, and you can delete the *Otherwise* part if needed by tapping on the ⊗ symbol in front of it.

The logic of *If... Otherwise... End If* is very simple.

> Check the condition inside the *If* part;
>
> and if that condition is true, then execute the Actions just following the *If* part (between *If* and *Otherwise*);
>
> but if that condition is not true (ie, false), then execute the Actions just following the *Otherwise* part (between *Otherwise* and *End If*).
>
> *End If* marks the end of the *If* construct.

Now tap on Input field just after *If.* A small menu pops up, and it will show you the familiar magic variables. Because we going to deal with a time, select *Current Date.* The variable *Current Date* will be populated in that field.

Remember that a Date object always includes both the date and the time in it (hence sometimes I will write it as Date/time).

In this case, we need to deal with time only because we are checking whether the time is before or after 12:00 PM. So, tap on the *Current Date* field, and you will see its properties/option to set as follows. At the bottom you can see the date and time format currently selected. It is like *9 Sep 2024 at 9:41AM*.

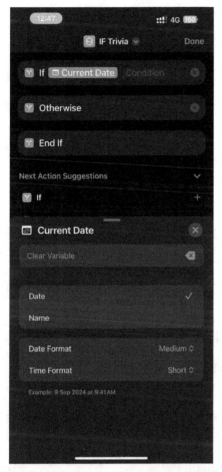

Tap on *Medium* in front of the *Date Format* and select *None*. This tell we are not interested in a date. The date string at the bottom shows how the current date/time string is now formatted (like *9:41PM*). Only time is included now.

You can experiment with the different time formats by selecting different format specifier by tapping on *Short* in front of the *Time Format* too (Try changing to *Medium,* and to *Long* and see how the time format changes). For our Shortcut, whatever time format will do.

Tap on the *Condition* field. You will see a list of condition operators in a menu – *is exactly, is not, has any value, does not have any value, contains, does not contain, begins with, ends with*. Select *contains*.

Anyway, what are these operators?

We are to check something and take a decision accordingly. In this case, we are checking on a date/time. What can you check with a date/time? Now think about it considering the above list of operators. Date/time could be compared as follows.

> The date <u>is</u> January 29, 2022
>
> The time <u>is</u> 23:42
>
> The time <u>is</u> no 12:23PM
>
> The time <u>contains</u> PM
>
> The date <u>does not contain</u> January

And so on. You can compare date/time in many different ways with those operators.

The list of operators changes in accordance with the type of the object in the *If* condition. In this case, it was *Current Date* (ie, a Date/time object) with the time part only (you disabled or removed the date part by setting date format to *None*).

To further check on this, long press on *Current Date* field, and select *Device Details* now. Now tap on the *condition* field, and you will have only two operators – *has any value* and *does not have any value*. Remember this fact.

Ok. Now revert to *Current Date* removing *Device Details*. Wait a second. Again tap on the *condition* field, and now you see a different list again. Why is that?

In the first occasion, you saw the list of operators for a Date/time object with date part disabled/removed. But when you changed it to *Device Details* and changed back to *Current Date*, the previous settings you set is reset. Now this list of operators is related to the Date/time object with both date and time parts included in it.

Ok. Ultimately you should have selected *Current Date* and set its *Date Format* to *None,* and selected *Contains* in the condition field.

Type in pm in the Text field, and tap *Done.* So, the Action should be read as "check if the Current Date (rather the current time in the Current Date object) contains pm in it"

What should it do if the time contains "pm" now? It should display on the screen "Good evening". Right?

To show something on screen, now let's insert the *Show Alert* Action.

The *Show Alert* Action is added to the end of the Actions list as usual. Drag it just under the *If* statement and just above the *Otherwise* statement. Change its prompt from *"Do you want to continue?"* to "Good evening".

So, if the time part contains PM, it means the time is after the noon. If the time does not contain PM, it will obviously contain AM. If it is AM, then we should alert "Good Morning".

So, the *If* construct checks if the condition contains pm, and if it does, it will execute the Actions just under the *If* statement which is to alert "Good evening".

If it is not pm, then it jumps to the *Otherwise* segment to execute the Actions just under the *Otherwise.*

So, insert another *Show Alert* Action, drag it just under the *Otherwise* statement, and change its variable to the string "Good morning".

Without adding the same Action again and again, you have an easy way to add an Action that has been already inserted. Duplicate the Action. Tap on the little Action symbol to the left of the Action name, and select *Duplicate* from the list. A copy/duplicate of the Action will be added immediately below it. It's an exact copy. Just drag it down under the *Otherwise* and change its variable to "Good morning".

That's it. Test the shortcut now. Nothing happens. Something wrong! Can you guess the error? It's the "pm" string. You must have entered it like pm or Pm.

Variables and text are case-sensitive.

So, you must mind capital simple letters; case matters. Type it in all capital as PM (because that's how it is in the time format), and test it again. It must work now.

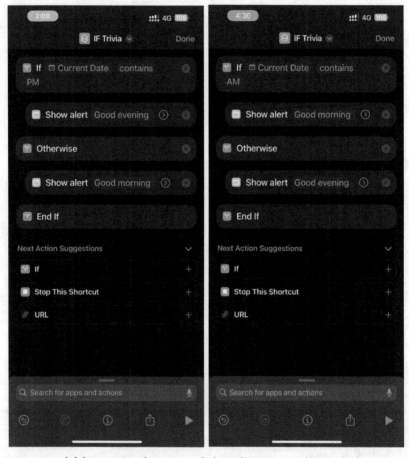

You could have implemented the Shortcut (above left image) in a different logic too (above right image).

Date

Date and time are important concepts both in real life and technology. Apple ecosystem has a smart Date object to deal with it. Let's have a peek into it.

You already know that Apple Date object includes both date and time in it. You can modify it to present the date part only, or the time part only. Or you can customize it whatever way you like it.

You have seen many date formats and time formats in daily life. We have two popular date formats – US and UK.

The UK date format is illustrated as dd/mm/yy or some other variations of it, like dd-mm-yy, dd/mm/yyyy, d/m/yy, etc. You may have hyphen or slash as the separator.

d (or dd) represents day, m (or mm) represents month, and yy (or yyyy) represents year. Why would you write d and m once or twice, and yy twice or four times?

d means the day is either single digit (if it is less than 10) or double digits (from 10 to 31), but dd always needs to be written in two digits like 01, 02, 09, 10, 11, 30, etc.

In the same way, m means the month is either single digit (if the month is from January to November) or two digits (if it is October, November or December), and mm always needs the month in two digits.

yy is short year like 81 (ie, 1981), and yyyy is long year like 1981.

d/m/yy – 2/3/81 (February 2, 1981), 21/3/81 (March 21, 1981)
dd/mm/yy – 02/03/1981 (February 2, 1981)
dd/mm/yyyy – 20/12/2021 (December 20, 2021)

The US date format is mm/dd/yy or any of its variants like m/d/yy, mm/dd/yyyy, etc.

You must give very serious consideration when you work with dates in your devices and messages. You may easily confuse the two date formats and miss very important situations. Believe me, it has occurred to me.

When you set up or customize your phone, tab, or computer, you usually have to select your country, and other locale details. Thereby you have set the date format too. You can change it in your device's settings. Mine is US date format, and therefore you will see dates in my examples in this book in the US date format.

Like the date, time also has several formats, but it is much easier to understand; no confusion at all.

> Time may be in 12 hour or 24 hour clock format. It may be as short as 9:41PM (in 12H), or 21:41 (in 24H) or as long as 9:41:23AM GMT+5.30. Sometimes the GMT offset is also written like +0530 without dots or colons.

> You know time is different from location to location. If it is 9.30PM now in Sri Lanka, it will be 4PM in the UK. Therefore, we have come to a consensus on a uniform time based on the GMT time.

> GMT time is the actual time on the Greenwich meridian that goes across the UK. The local time (the time at your place) is taken with respect to the GMT now. Because Sri Lanka is +5.30, it means I have to add 5 hours and 30 minutes to the GMT time if I want to get my local time in Sri Lanka.

> Every country has a GMT offset like -3.00, +7.00, etc. What's your country's GMT offset?

Apple Date has several standard date formats; it changes in accordance with the specific formats you choose for the time part and the date part. The following are a few examples.

2024-09-09, 9:41AM
2024-09-09, 9:41:34AM
9 Sep 2024 at 9:41AM
9 September 2024 at 9:41AM
Mon, 09 Sep 2024 09:41:00 +0530   (RFC2822 format)
2024-09-09T09:41:00+05:30   (ISO 8601 format)

The real power of the Date object comes with the customization of the format. You can create/customize your own date/time format. For that, we need the following format keys. Remember that case (simple capital distinction) matters.

> y – year.
> > yy (81) or
> > yyyy (1981)
>
> M – month.
> > M (eg: 3) or
> > MM (eg: 03) or
> > MMM (eg: Mar) or
> > MMMM (eg: March)
>
> e – day of the week.
> > e (eg: 2) or
> > ee (eg: 02) or
> > eee (eg: Tue) or
> > eeee (eg: Tuesday)
>
> d – date.
> > d (eg: 7) or
> > dd (eg: 07)
>
> h – hour in 12H clock.
> > h (eg: 1) or
> > hh (eg: 01)
>
> H – hour in 24H clock.
> > H (eg: 13) or
> > HH (eg: 13)
>
> m – minute.
> > m (eg: 8) or
> > mm (eg: 08)
>
> s – second.
> > s (eg: 4) or
> > ss (eg: 04)
>
> a – AM/PM

z – GMT offset in the +5:50 format
Z – GMT offset in the +0530 format

Now combine the above format keys in a string to make your own date/time format. Have a look at the following examples. Study carefully the subtle difference between the second and the third examples.

eee, MMM dd, yyyy   eg: Wed, Feb 04, 1981
MM/dd/yy, hh:mma   eg: 03/21/24, 11:32PM
MM/dd/yy, hh:mm a   eg: 03/21/24, 11:32 PM
H   eg: 15 (only the hour in 24H clock)

Improving If Action

I want to improve the above Shortcut a little bit. I want it to greet "Good afternoon" too. The logic is to greet Good morning in the morning, and greet Good afternoon if the time is between the noon and 3pm, and otherwise say Good evening.

Looks pretty simple to do. Think about it; you may come up with several solutions.

Unfortunately, Apple Shortcuts still does not give us logical operators (AND, OR, NOT) within the If condition, as in general programming. If it did, the task would have been a piece for cake. The logic would be like:

If the time string contains AM, then say Good morning;

Else (Otherwise) if the time string has 12 or 13 or 14 in the 24H clock time, then say Good afternoon;

Else (Otherwise) in all other cases, say Good evening.

However, Shortcuts does not support any logical operator. If you possibly did not understand anything about logical operators, just forget it. You don't need it.

So, we have to repeatedly use *If* constructs. The logic goes like:

If the time string contains AM, then say Good morning;

Otherwise if the time string begins with 12, say Good afternoon;

Otherwise if the time string begins with 13, say Good afternoon;

Otherwise if the time string begins with 14, say Good afternoon;

Otherwise in all other cases, say Good evening.

Because with each *If* comes its own *End If,* you will see a several End If's at the end.

In the device (system), date and time is stored in a standard way; that internal format does not change.

When you access that system date, it can be displayed in a number of formats as we discussed earlier. So, you may display it in 12-hour format or 24-hour format. In my logic above, I have used both of these formats, and it does not matter to the device because the system always keeps time in its own standard internal date/time format.

There is a lot of redundancy (the same Good evening greeting three times, for example) in this type of coding. Generally, in programming, it is highly denounced to program like this. It is highly counter-productive. I don't know why Apply had not offered us logical operators so we could have achieved it much easier and faster.

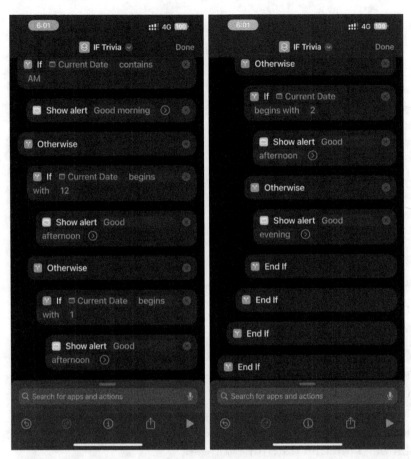

However, we can simplify the Shortcut. We are going to use a very versatile and useful Action called *Match Text*.

Let's modify the Shortcut. Delete all the Actions except the first one (keep the first *If* Action). Tap on the ⊗ in front of the second *If* construct. It would ask whether you want to delete some other Actions with it. It asks so because we have inserted several Actions (in different levels) within that Action.

You can only delete that *If* construct and its *Otherwise* and *End If* parts if you select *Keep Actions* from the list. Then the other Actions will remain.

But in this modification, we will delete all of them, so select *Delete* Actions. You will be left with the first *If* Action with its *Otherwise* and *End If* parts only.

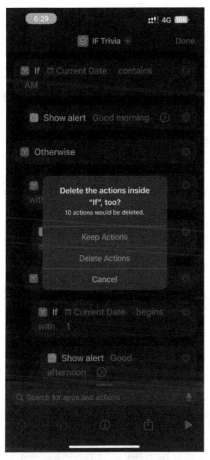

Insert the Action *Match Text* now. Drag it just under *Otherwise* and just above *End if*.

Match Text Action takes in some arbitrary text and extract a specific string. It's like you look up a word in a dictionary. The real magic here is that you can extract a specific text/string based on a pattern.

Think, for example, you are given some text and asked to look for an email address in it. You know how an email address (ie, sumith@tekcroach.top) looks like (you know the email address format). That format in your head is the pattern indeed. In your head, you see it like *"several characters followed by an @ and then followed by some other text and then a dot and followed by a short string like com, us, top, lk"*.

The *Match Text* Action must be given both the original string, and the pattern. If it finds some text in the original string matching that pattern, then it extracts that piece of matched text and outputs it. You can retrieve and access that output later in other Actions as usual. If it does not find any matching text, it outputs nothing (empty).

Tap on Text field to select the original string. Select *Current Date*. Change the date/time format to include only the hour in 24 hour clock because we are interested only in the rough time of the day (hour is sufficient). How to do that?

Tap on *Current Date* in the match Action. Then tap on the *Date Format* and select *Custom*. Then you will see something like *EEE, dd MMM yyy HH:mm:ss Z*. Can you visualize the date format of this? It's a date/time like *Wed, 04 February 1981 20:32:00 +0530*. Delete it altogether, and write H in it. Just H. Press *return* in the keyboard.

Then tap on *[0-9a-zA-Z]* field. It is the default pattern. We will learn about patterns in a while, so for now change it to (12|13|14).

Then add another *If* Action and drag it just under the match Action.

Change the condition of this new *If* Action to *Matches*, if it is not already set to *Matches* automatically.

Change its operation to *has any value*.

The *has any value* operator simply returns/outputs True if it can find any text or value returned by that Action. So, if the match Action could find/extract a string out of the input text, it will output that extracted string through its *Matches* variable. Then *has any value* operator will output True.

If the match Action could not extract/find a text according to the pattern, then its output variable will contain nothing. In that case, *has any value* operator will output False.

Ok. Now duplicate the *Show alert Good morning*, and drag it just under the *If Matches has any value*.

Change its Good morning to `Good afternoon`.

Duplicate either *Show alert Good morning* or *Show alert Good evening*, and drag it just under the last *Otherwise*.

Change its Good afternoon to `Good evening`.

Try to understand the logic of the Shortcut yourself.

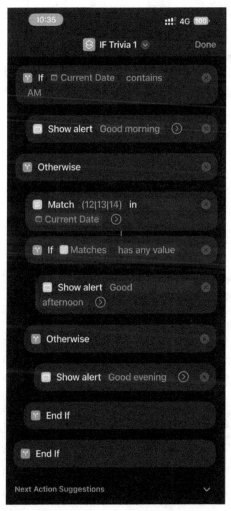

We access the *Current Date* twice during the lifetime of the Shortcut. There is a subtlety here because the *Current Date* is a special magic variable. Every time it is called/referenced/accessed, you get the real-time (or live) time of your device. So, there is always a very teeny tiny time difference between its first calling and the second calling. In our example, we do not care at all about this tiny difference. But you must remember this fact!

Match Text and Regular Expressions (REGEX)

We used the *Match Text* Action in our previous example. It is very very interesting and powerful one. As you now know it gets two inputs – one input is the original text on which the second input which is the pattern is applied. If it finds a suitable substring matching the pattern, then it will output that matched substring/text.

The pattern is the magic portion of this Action. The pattern is officially/formally known as a **regular expression (regex)**. Regex is a crucial tool in any programming. Actually, regex is a standard on its own. You can learn about regex from the Internet. Therefore, once you learn it, you can apply it everywhere every day.

However, every programming language or tool that utilizes regex including Apple Shortcuts for that matter might not implement the whole regex standard. It may omit some parts/functions.

In regex, you write a pattern or regular expression using a cryptic notation. Don't worry; it's not hard to learn or remember that notation. You must remember the following few notations and points.

1. If you write an individual letter, it is considered as it is. For example, **a** is literally considered as **a** (not **A**); **b** as **b** (not **B**); **k** as **k** (not **K**); **A** as **A** (not **a**); **T** as **T** (not **t**); **4** as **4**; **@** as **@**; **#** as **#**; **_** as **_**; **%** as **%**; **&** as **&**; **=** as **=**.

2. Letters are case-sensitive. So, **a** is not **A**, and **B** is not **b**.

3. You can write a string of letters/characters like **abc**, **Sumith**, **1234**, etc.

4. \d – represents any single digit (from 0 to 9).

   \D – represents any single character except a digit.

5. \w – represents any single alphanumeric character.

   Alphanumeric includes all the alphabetical characters (in both capital and simple letters) and digits (from 0 to 9).

   In English, this includes simple letters from a to z, the capital letters from A to Z, and the digits 0 to 9. It does not include space.

   \W – represents any single letter that is neither alphabetic nor digit. This even includes the space.

6. \s – any single whitespace.

   Whitespace is simply the space between letters or words. You write space with the spacebar key in the keyboard.

   There are special types of space too – **tab, newline**. These are all carry-over from the old typewriter.

   Tab is a a group of consecutive spaces (usually 4 normal spaces). It has its own cryptic character \t too.

   New line is as the name itself means the signal to go to the next line. Its cryptic character is \n. This is what happens when you press the Enter key on the keyboard.

   \s represents any kind of these whitespaces.

   \S – represents any single character that is not a whitespace.

7. **.** (dot or period) – represents any character. This includes alphabetical characters (both simple and capital), digits, whitespace, punctuation marks, special characters like @, #, &, etc.

8. Because we used the dot for a special purpose (to denote any character), we no longer cannot interpret the dot <u>literally</u> as it is (in the meaning of point 1 above).

   If you want to literally interpret the dot, use **\.** instead. The dot is immediately preceded with a backslash (\).

   This practice of immediately preceding with backslash is called "**escaping**". So, in this case, we escaped the period/dot.

9. ***** - this is preceded by a character. It means that immediately preceding character can exist 0 or many times.

   Now you must be able to understand that you cannot literally use the asterisk (*), and it has to be escaped like * if you intend to literally interpret it.

10. **+** - this is preceded by a character. It means that the immediately preceding character can exist 1 or many times.

    If you want to interpret + literally, escape it like **\+**.

11. **?** – this is also preceded by a character. It means that the immediately preceding character can exist 0 or 1 time. We may as well say the preceding character is optional.

    You can escape it by **\?**.

12. **[ ]** – a pair of square brackets must include one or more characters in it, like *[abc]*, *[a-z]*, *[3-9]*. It then represents

any single character out of the set of characters within the bracket. For example, *[abc]* means *a* or *b* or *c*; nothing else allowed.

What if you needed to say any single character out of the 26 English letters? Would you write it like *[abcdefghijklmnopqrstuvwxyz]*? Of course, you could write it like so. But there's a short way.

You write a range with a hyphen like **[a-z]**. Then all the consecutive letters from a to z are specified. If it is *[c-g]*, it means one of *c,d,e,f,g*, and it could have also been written in expanded and boring way like *[cdefg]*. *[3-7]* is equivalent to *[34567]*.

You can have several ranges in the same bracket too. For example, **[a-zA-Z]** means all the English letters of both cases. **[a-zA-Z0-9]** means the whole alphanumeric character base. It is thus equivalent to \w.

This notation included the possible characters. You can use this bracket notation to exclude characters also. Just precede the content with ^, like *[^abc]*, *[^A-Z]*. [^abc] means any character except a or b or c. *[^A-Z]* means any character except capital English letters.

13. **{n}** – preceded by a character. n is an integer. It says n times of the immediately preceding character exist. For example, *t{3}* is equivalent to *ttt*.

    {m,n} – similar to {n}, but this time the preceding character can multiplies m to n times. For example, *k{2,4}* may represent *kk* or *kkk* or *kkkk*.

14. **^** - this **hat** sign which is prefixed to a string indicates that the matched substring must be at the very beginning of the original text. For example, *^ed+* may represent *education*, *editor*, and so on, but it cannot represent

looked, medical, and so on.

This use of ^ is clearly different from its application in point 12 above. In the point 12, the ^ was inside a [ ].

15. **$** - this **dollar** sigh which is postfixed to a string indicates that the matched substring must end with this specific string. For example, *\w+ed$* may represent *liked, raced*, and so on, but cannot represent *editor, medical*, and so on.

16. **( )** – you can use parentheses to group a string. For example, *(abc)* just means *abc*, and *(234)* means *234*. Noting exciting! However, the real power of it comes when you use it with the **pipe operator** (|). Pipe operator is the vertical bar. It is interpreted as an OR operation. For example, *(abc|def)* means *either abc or def. (cat|dog|fish)* means *cat or dog or fish*.

17. You must understand that we cannot literally interpret (,), [,], {, } because we used them in special meanings. So, you must escape them like \(, \), \[, \], \{, \} if you want to include them in the pattern in the literal meaning. In the same token, the hyphen (-) and the plus sign (+) must be escaped like \- and \+ respectively.

You can mix and combine all the above points together to create any complex regex pattern. Let's take a few examples.

1. If you want to write a pattern to identify/extract a 10-digit telephone number, how would you write it? It must not falsely identify a telephone number with less than or more than 10 digits. It should not include hyphens or parentheses or spaces in it.

   \d{10}

   So, a telephone number like *0781027994* matches with

this regex, but *078 102 7994* or *(078)1027994* or *078-1027994* won't match with the pattern.

2. What if you wanted to include the other formats of telephone numbers mentioned in the previous paragraph?

   \(?\d{3}\)?(|\-)?\d{3}( )?\d{4}

   Can you analyze the above pattern part by part?

   (i) The first part is \(. It is just the opening parenthesis. We can't directly write it as (because the parentheses have a special function in regex, and therefore you must escape it with \ if you want its literal meaning.

   It is followed by a question mark. If the question mark were not there, that means the number must always start with a (. Then we are limited only to numbers like *(078).......* Therefore, we make the (optional by appending a ?.

   (ii) The next part is \d{3}. This means any 3 digits. That's very simple.

   (iii) The next part is \)?. I hope now you can understand what it signifies. It says there is an optional closing parenthesis.

   (iv) Next is (|-)? part. It says there must be optionally either a single whitespace or a hyphen.

   Sometimes you might not notice that there is a single space between (and |, but there is.

   I could have included \s instead of a single space there, but I didn't because I wanted the phone number to have only one space if it happens to include space.

You may as well enclose the single space with parentheses to make it more prominent, like ( ). Now you can see there is a space between (and).

(v) *d{3}* part was found earlier too. You now know what it means – 3 digits.

(vi) *( )?* part simply means an optional space. This time I used parentheses to enclose the single whitespace for clarity.

(vii) *\d{4}* part denotes four more digits.

3. Let's write a simple regex pattern to identify an email address. This pattern can identify email addresses in the format of *sumith@tekcroach.top, sumith.lk@tekcroach.top, sumith43@tekcroach.top, sumith+shortcuts@tekcroach.top, sumith@shortcuts.tekcroach.top.*

   There are a few conditions too. The email must start with an English letter. The userid and domain part can include the hyphen and the period a number of times, but no consecutive periods or hyphens shall exist. All the letters must be in lower case (actually case does not matter in email address).

   ^[a-z]([a-z0-9]+(\./\-)?)+[a-z0-9]+\+?[a-z0-9]+@ ([a-z0-9]+(\./\-)?)+[a-z0-9]+\.[a-z]{2,4}$

Trivial Repeat

This Shortcut example is created just to let you experience what *repeat* does. I think it is important first to grasp the fundamental meaning or working before you are going to use it productively in a complex task.

Create a new Shortcut with a suitable name.

Insert the *Repeat* Action (not the *Repeat with Each*).

Tap on the repeat *time* field and set the number of repetitions.

Insert a *Show Alert* Action. Delete the default content, and insert the *Repeat Index* variable, and a colon (:), and `Hi there`.

That's it. Test it now.

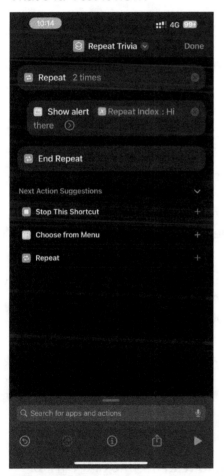

The *Show Alert* Action is within the *Repeat* construct. I set the number of repetitions to 2 times. That means the repeat Action is going execute whatever inside it two times.

In this example, there is only one Action inside it, and therefore you will get alerts two times.

The alert itself contains two parts in it. One is simply the literal string part which is ": Hi there". The other part is the variable *Repeat Index*.

Repeat Item and Repeat Index

Repeat (and its cousin *Repeat with Each*) always offers two important variables – *Repeat Index* and *Repeat Item*.

Repeat Item is the variable which contains the actual item content.

Repeat Index is the index value of that item in the list. The first item will have a *Repeat Index* of *1*, the second item will have *2*, the third will have *3*, and so on.

> Remember that the Shortcut's indices always start from 1, not zero. If you are possibly into computer programming with C/C++/Arduino or that sort of programming languages, indices start with 0 in those languages.

In this specific example, we did not have a content/data to work on repeatedly. But usually, we work *repeat* on a list of items. For example, it can be a list of names where each row has a new name like:

> *Sumith Wanni Arachchige*
> *Lakdini de Seram*
> *Kavindu Kasun*
> *Hashitha Dasun*
> *Ahasna Goonethilake*

If you employ a *repeat* Action to read this file of the list of names, the repeat will start reading the first line first.

In its first round/iteration, the *Repeat Item* will contain *Sumith Wanni Arachchige*, and the *Repeat Index* will be *1*. The Actions can use those variables.

In the second iteration, the *Repeat Item* now possesses *Lakdini de Seram* and the *Repeat Index* is *2*.

I think you can follow this pattern of working.

In the Apple ecosystem, you have many Actions which result in a list of items like *Split Text, Filter Files, Get Playlist, Find Reading List Items, List,* and so on.

Each of these Actions return a list of items, and you can use a *repeat* Action to work on each of the list item in the list one by one in a loop.

The list might contain hundreds of thousands of items, or a couple of items, or only one item, or else no item at all. *Repeat* Actions take care of any of these situations.

Trivial Repeat with Each

Let's explore the *Repeat with Each* Action, now that we have a good working knowledge of its younger brother *Repeat*. This also iterates or loops, but this will loop on a list of items and will loop until each of the list item is traversed.

In the case of *Repeat,* it looped a fixed number of times only. That's a big difference!

Create a Shortcut like below. Now you must be able to create a Shortcut just by visually going through it.

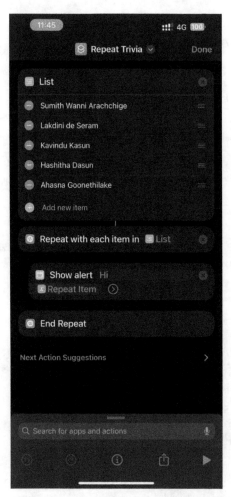

I hope you could do it. Ok, here's how it is done.

Insert the *List* Action first. It will automatically include literals *One* and *Two* as its list items. Tap on *One*, delete it, and write a name. Do the same for *Two*.

Tap on *Add new item*, and enter the other list items. Then tap on *Done*.

List is actually an Action which lets us create a list like that. Then, we could use that list of items in the Shortcut.

If you want, you can insert a variable as a list item. In our example, we entered a few names (text or literals), but you could select a variable (and the content held by that variable will be available through the *Repeat Item* then).

Then insert a *Repeat with Each* Action. It will automatically populate its field with the *List* variable which is the magic variable offered by the preceding *List* Action. If not, select *List* variable.

Finally add a *Show Alert* Action and change its field to string Hi and then followed by *Repeat Item* variable.

That's it. Test it. It will alert you several times. How many times exactly? In my Shortcut, it did five times. Why 5 times? Because there were five items (ie, 5 names) in the list. It means the repeat Action repeated or looped five times. It looped as long as there were items in the list.

Email with an Attachment

We are going to create a Shortcut that lets you email a selected file. We will make several versions of it until we get a useful Shortcut.

Create a Shortcut with the name Email Attachment.

Insert the *Select File* Action.

This will let you select a file (any file) in your system. You can browse and select a file as you normally browse the device's file system.

Tap on the little arrow head ⊘ and the Action will expand to show you its properties. Toggle the *Select Multiple* setting on. If you do not turn this on, you could select only one file. If you toggle it on, you could select any number of files.

> Actually, you cannot send any number of attachments in real life because your email service may have imposed a limit. Usually, they do have limits.

Insert a *Repeat with Each* Action. It will automatically have populated its field with *File* variable; if not, select it now. If you select a several files, then the repeat Action will loop several times.

Then add Send Email Action. Drag it inside the repeat Action.

Send Email Action can send an email on your behalf. It basically has three fields – *Message, Recipients*, and *Subject.* I hope these fields are obvious to you.

Message means the body of the email (including attachments, if any);

the *subject* is the subject of the email:

and the *Recipients* is one or more recipient email addresses.

Tap on its first field (*Message*), and you can type in any text you want. You can simply write anything (some simple text), or you can import a nicely formatted text into this too (via a variable). Or else, you can import a file (as an attachment) into this too.

In this example, we are going to include a file as an attachment. What you select in the *Select File* Action are going to be attached here as files.

Select *Repeat Item* in this field.

The scenario is that the user selects several files, but the repeat Actions now has only one file in this particular iteration, and that file is now attached to the email; and in the next iteration it will send another email with the next file, and so on.

Test it. You will get a **Privacy screen** like below right image. Select *Always Allow* or *Allow Once* to keep it running. If you selected *Don't Allow*, the script stops right away.

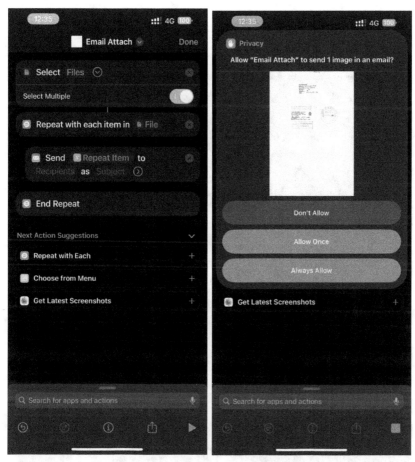

This sort of privacy screen will pop up whenever you are going to run a Shortcut for the first time on your device and it is going to email, text, call, and so on. It's a good security measure implemented by the Apple ecosystem.

If you selected *Always Allow* above, the device won't ask again. The Shortcut remembers your decision. However, if you later think you must revoke that permission, can you do that? Of course, you can; you are the boss!

In the Shortcut editor screen, tap on the ⓘ button. Then you will see three tabs at the top of the new screen – *Details*, *Privacy*, and *Setup*.

You have already seen and worked with the settings in the *Details* tab in our previous Shortcuts. Now tap on the *Privacy* tab. You will see something like below left image. If you had not run the Shortcut as yet, then the screen will be like below right.

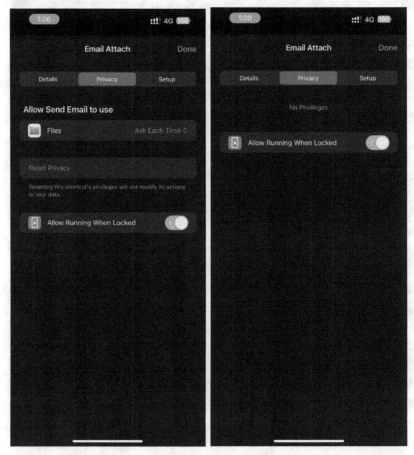

If you had run the Shortcut at least once, and had selected *Always Allow*, then the permission in front of Files will be showing *Always Allow*, but otherwise, it will be set to *Ask Each Time*. You can tap on *Ask Each Time* field and select *Don't Allow* if you want to stop the Action.

You can tap on *Reset Privacy* to reset this pane as if you have never run this Shortcut on your device before.

At the bottom, you can see *Allow Running When Locked* option/setting. It is normally enabled. If you disable it, as the name itself suggests your Shortcut will not be able to run when the device is locked.

In the end, when you run the Shortcut, you will get the usual Compose New Email window now. The file is already attached to it. You can now enter one or more recipient addresses, a suitable subject, some text, if you want, in the body. Then send the email. This part you have to do manually, but we can automate it too. Bear with me.

Let's tweak this Shortcut a little by little.

Write something in the *Subject* field in the *Send Email* Action. Therefore, this text will automatically be placed in your email subject line.

Write your own email address in the *Recipients* field. If you want, you can include several email addresses here.

> Remember that most email services have imposed many limits/restrictions on their services. For example, you may not include any number of email addresses at once. There might be an upper limit like 20 or so.

You can even enter some text in the *Message* field along with the *Repeat Item* variable. If you enter this text just before the *Repeat Item*, the text will appear first and then the attachment at the bottom. You can enter text and press the Enter key to go to new lines too. Fiddle with it. I have entered `Hi` there as the first line, and then `This is the second line.` as the second line.

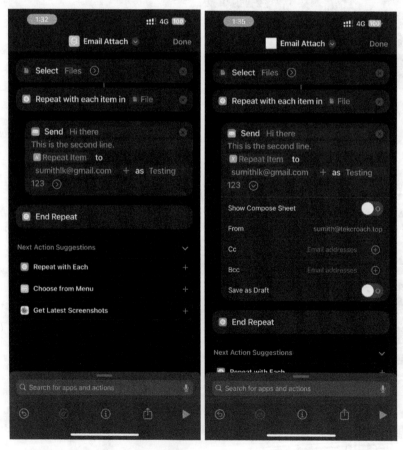

Then expand the properties of *Send Email* Action. Toggle off the *Show Compose Sheet* button. When this is enabled, you will be shown the usual Compose New Email window. When this is off, the email will be sent unseen to you.

As you can see, there are a few other options that you might want to set, like *CC* (Carbon Copy), *BCC* (Blind Carbon Copy), *Save as Draft*. Set them as you prefer.

This Shortcut will email you a file instantly. It is really useful now. Sometimes, we email something to ourselves for some safety or archival purpose.

> Another warning: some email services will not allow you to send some types of files (especially executable files like *.exe*). If it fails to send an email with such a file being attached, it is not the fault of your Shortcut.

When you run the above Shortcut, you will get another privacy concern window. Why this time? Well, you have run a Shortcut that is going to communicate (ie, email) without your notice. It is indeed a privacy concern. It does not show you any email compose window this time. So, it asks for your permission. You can change your permissions of a Shortcut as described a moment ago.

This Shortcut is really annoying because it sends a separate email for each attachment. We designed it this way to show you how to use repeat Action. But you can remove that annoyance by removing the repeat Action and attaching all the files in one mail instead. How to do that?

First remove the *Repeat with Each* action. Select *Keep Actions* in the popped-up alert. This will keep the *Send Email Action* as it is.

Now you will see one of its fields in <u>red</u>; *Repeat Item* variable is shown in red.

Something shown in red color means something wrong with it.

What is actually wrong with the *Repeat Item*? It is an invalid variable now. It belonged to the repeat Action, and we deleted the repeat Action.

The *Repeat Item* should no longer exist. So, remove it. Tap on it and select *Clear Variable*; it's gone. Good.

However, there is no files attached to the body now. Previously the file was attached via the *Repeat Item* variable. Now you have to include another variable to attach the selected variables. It's very easily doable. Tap on the small empty space in the field (just before the *to*), and select the *File* variable.

The *File* is the magic variable offered by the *Select File* Action. When you select one or more files, those selected files are included as a list of files inside this variable.

Ok, now test the Shortcut. It works! It's now very much useful a Shortcut.

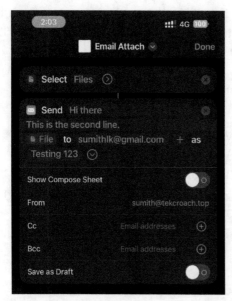

Mail Merge

Mail merge is traditionally a very handy Word Processing tool/feature.

Sometimes, you would have to write the same letter to a number of people, and only the name and address are different. The rest of the document remains the same.

You could write a separate document (with copy-pasting) to each of the recipient, or you could use the mail merge facility.

The name, address, and some other structured details (like the contact number, the email, the joined_date, etc) are saved in a database. Then you write the document with variables/fields in the relevant parts in the document, and link those fields to the relevant fields in the database.

Let's see an example. The following is a part of a document to be sent to Sumith.

> *Dear Sumith*
>
> *I am pleased to let you know that we have launched a new book on Amazon bookstore. I have already sent you an email to your sumith@tekcroach.top and hope to get a reply from you soon. Blah blah blah...*

Let's say you need to send this same email to Shane, Lakdini, and a few hundred people. Imagine how much of a pain it would have been if you were to write a separate letter (even with copy-pasting) to each one of them.

What you can do is to include variables/fields in the relevant places in the above document. Then the above document would be something like below.

> *Dear #FirstName*
>
> *I am pleased to let you know that we have launched a new book on Amazon bookstore. I have already sent you an email to your #email and hope to get a reply from your soon. Blah blah blah...*

#FirstName and *#email* are fields or variables (placeholders for the actual content). This document with the fields is known as a **template**.

You also create a simple database with those details where you store first name, email, and other pertinent details of each person.

Then you link each of the fields in the template to the related field in the database. Then the word processing software will automatically create separate documents for each person replacing the fields with the specific relevant data.

It can create thousands of such documents (and even print them) for you within a few seconds. It saves you hours of boring work.

Well, that's enough on traditional mail merge. You can learn more about it, if you will. I will briefly touch on mailing lists now.

A mailing list is kind of a service where you send the same email to thousands or even millions of (subscribed) users.

If you mass-email without the prior consent of the recipients, it is known as **spamming**, and spamming is an illegal practice.

With this Shortcut, you can send an email with attachments, if any, to a number of email addresses. Moreover, the email addresses, in this example, must already be in a database (in CSV format).

CSV stands for **Comma Separated Values**. It is also known as **Comma Delimited Values**. It is an extremely simple and useful database format. Anyone can create a csv file even with the dumbest text editor (like Notepad in Windows, TextEdit in mac).

You just write text separated by commas. Then save the file with the csv extension. That's it.

For example, create a file named *names.csv*. Its content may be like:

Sumith,Lakdini,Hashitha,Kavindu,Ahasna

We usually take each text delimited by a comma as a separate data item. So, *Sumith, Lakdini, Hashitha, Kavindu, Ahasna* are all individual data items.

We must have a mechanism to separate out these individual data items in Shortcut. That is, we need to split this long comma-delimited string into smaller data items. We have the *Split Text* Action for that.

The *Split Text* Action takes in the long string and chop it at every place where a special character is found. Along with the long string to be split, we must pass to it the special character. Usually that special character can be space, newline (it is the character generated when you press the Enter key on the keyboard), a comma, a period, or whatever character you desire, for that matter.

In our example, comma is going to be the special character. Then the split Action will split the long string into smaller chunks at each comma, and will output a list of individual names.

Before creating the mail merge, let's practice using *Split Text* with csv files first. Let's create another trivial Shortcut.

First creates a csv file with some comma delimited text. I go with the following. Save it in your device. I saved it as *names.csv.* Open it by tapping on it to see if it works well.

Sumith,Lakdini,Hashitha,Kavindu,Ahasna

Insert a *Select File* Action first to select/load the csv file into the Shortcut as usual.

Insert a *Split Text* Action next. It will automatically have the magic variable File filled in. Tap on *New Lines* to change it to *Custom,* and then type in a comma in the Custom Separator field. Press *Done.*

This will separate the above comma delimited text to *Sumith, Lakdini, Hashitha, Kavindu,* and *Ahasna.*

If you were to extract each line inside a file, you could set the separator field to *New Lines.* Then the *Split Text* will split each line into separate data. Consider, for example, the following poem with a few lines.

> *Twinkle twinkle little star*
> *How I wonder what you are*
> *Up above the world so high*
> *Like a diamond in the sky*

New Lines separator will break the above text into four individual lines – *Twinkle twinkle little star, How I wonder what you are, Up above the world so high,* and *Like a diamond in the sky.*

If you set it to *Spaces*, then the long string is split in places where space is found. With this space separator the above poem will have been chopped into individual words like *Twinkle, twinkle, little, star, How, I, wonder, what, you, are, Up, above, the, world, so, high, Like, a, diamond, in, the,* and *sky.*

If you set it to Every Character, then it will split the long string into each individual character. With this separator, the above poem will be chopped into each individual character like, *T, w, i, n, k, l, e, (space), t, w, i, n, k, l, e, (space), l, i, t, t, l, e, s, t, a, r, \n, H, o, w,* and so on. Here, spaces and the newline (\n) characters are also counted in.

If you had content separated by * instead of comma, like *Sumith*Lakdini*Hashitha*Kavindu*Ahasna,* then you could have set the separator field to *. Now, this file is not a comma separated value file, but rather an "asterisk separated value" file.

Likewise, you may have so many varieties of special-character-delimited-value files.

Now test it. You are asked to select a file. Select the csv file you created. I selected my *names.csv* file, and the result viewer inside the Shortcut editor window will show me the result.

We have seen this result viewer in our previous Shortcuts too. It's the high time to appreciate its importance. In the Shortcut creation stage, it shows you the result of the last Action.

You can check if the Actions (coding) so far work. Read the result to see if the intended output is obtained. Depending on the result data, you can view the result in several different ways. For example, the two following screenshots show one result in a card-stack, and the other as a list.

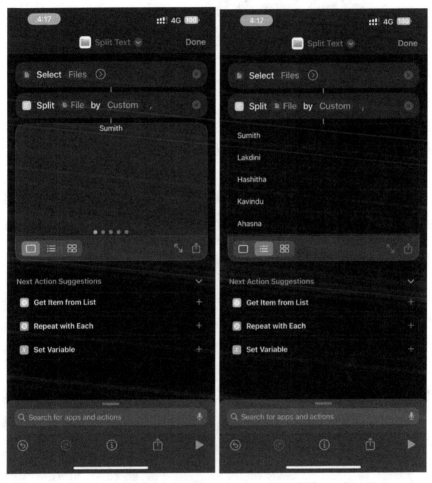

Now we know that the csv file was successfully split. Let's practice a little further with this Shortcut.

Add a *Repeat with Each Item* Action. Its field will have been populated with the magic variable *Split Text* automatically. If not, set it to *Split Text* variable.

Then add a *Show Alert* Action, drag it inside the repeat, and set its field to *Repeated Item*.

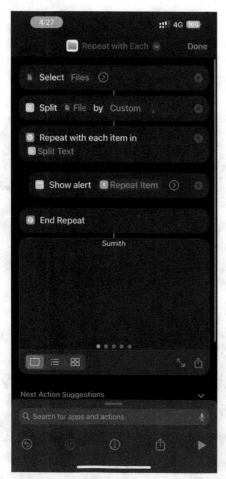

Ok, you can experiment and explore as much as you wish. Go wild! You will be okay. It cannot harm you or your device.

Let's now create the mail merge Shortcut proper.

Insert a *Show Alert* Action. Change its field to `Select a comma delimited email list file` or some other sensible text.

You can delete characters one at a time by tapping on the Delete/Backspace key on your keyboard.

Or if you double tap on a word, the entire word is selected and if you triple tap on something, the entire text is selected; then you can delete the entire word or the text at once.

This alerts/says to the user that he has to select a csv file which has the email address delimited by a comma.

Insert a *Select File* Action. It will automatically be populated with *Files* variable. If not, set it to *Files*. This Action selects the csv file.

Make sure to set its *Select Multiple* toggle switch to off (expand by tapping on the arrow head to see the setting). You don't need to select multiple files here – only one csv file.

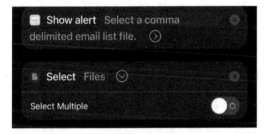

Insert again a *Show Alert* Action, and change its field to `Select one or more files to attach.`

It says to select one or more files that you are going to attach to the user later. The ultimate purpose of this Script is to email the attachment(s) to a group of email addresses.

Insert again a *Select File* Action. Toggle on its *Select Multiple* property.

Insert the *Ask for Input* Action now. It has two fields that you must fill in.

This Action will ask for you to enter in the subject that you want as the subject of your email.

Ask for Input Action prompts you to type in something at the run-time. What you enter in here gets output as a magic variable.

You can type in a string/text, a number, a URL, a date or time. Tap on the first field of the Action to specify what sort of input *Ask for Input* is expecting you to enter.

Select *Text* from this list. It specifies you must enter in a string/text.

The other field (*prompt*) is the prompt string. What you write in it is displayed within the prompt. Type in something like `Enter the subject`.

Insert another *Ask for Input* Action or you may duplicate the previous Action. This is going to be the text that you want in the email body along with the attachment(s).

Change its first field to *Text*, and set the second field to `Enter the email body` or something like that.

Now add a *Split Text* Action to split the csv file content into individual email addresses. Warning: You are going to get into a trouble!

As usual you change its *New Lines* field (separator field) to *Custom* and then type in a comma.

What should be in its first field? Currently it is set to *Provided Input* (anyway, *Provided Input* is the magic variable of an *Ask for Input* Action). But we have to split the csv file, not just "any provided input". Long press on it, and you will get a list of variables. What is your best guess?

No clear idea, I Know. Maybe the *File* variable? Well, don't select any variable here for now.

We know that it must be the output (magic) variable of the first *Select File* Action. The "default" name of a Select File Action is *File*.

The problem is that we have two *Select File* Actions in our Shortcut. There is ambiguity here – two Actions with the same output variable name!

There are great solutions in situations like this.

First solution is to visually select the magic variable.

Long press on the relevant field (*Provided Input*) again, and tap on *Select Variable* option. You will get a screen like this. All the variables are shown in blue color.

Now you know what variable is your one. It must be the variable named File – the first *File* (the one with the arrow 1). Tap on that first *File*. That's it.

However, still it's not visually clear what specific *File* variable you have selected. If you probably tapped on the second *File* variable, still the split Action would be showing just *File*. Internally the Shortcut knows which specific variable it is referencing, but you can't.

Maybe you have a doubt whether you had selected the correct variable. How to know which specific magic variable it is referencing to? There is a way.

Tap on the *File* variable. You will see a variable property settings panel. Tap on *Reveal Action* button.

It will lightly highlight the specific Action to which the magic variable belongs; ambiguity vanishes. You now know which is which.

Yet, it is still not elegant. You want to make it visually unambiguous too. You can do it.

Rename Variables!

Yes, you can rename the magic variables.

First visually select the correct magic variable as we did earlier. Then rename it with a suitable unique name. How to rename a variable?

Tap on the variable name again, and you will get the variable property settings panel as shown in the previous image. Can you see a field named *Variable Name*? It already has *File* as its name. You tap on it and rewrite something. I'll rename it to `Comma Delimited Emails`.

Yes, in Shortcuts you can have variable names with spaces (usually, you can't have spaces in variable names in computer programming). And, in Shortcuts you can have several variables with the same name too (but it's not a good thing).

Add a *Repeat with Each* Action. It will automatically have its field filled in with *Split Text* which is the output variable of the split Action. That's correct, and therefore leave it.

Insert a *Send Email* Action, and drag it inside the repeat Action.

The Action's first field now gets populated wrongly; we'll modify it in a moment. You see, Apple's guesses are not always right! You are the boss and you must be in control, not Apple.

We have met this *Send Email* Action before. You must fill in the three fields of it with appropriate variables or content. Think for a moment yourself, and you can know what you should do.

Well, long press on *Recipients* field, and select *Repeat Item*. *Split Text* is the output of the split Action. It is where the email addresses live. The repeat Action iterates through this list one by one.

Likewise, long press on *Subject*, and select WHAT? Guess it. It must be the output of the first *Ask for* Input Action. Right? Because we have two ask for Actions (ask for variables are named *Provided Input* by default), you have to visually select the first one (follow the same steps we learned a moment ago).

Well, let's make it more elegant by renaming this *Provided Input* variable to something like Subject.

At last, we must enter two data items in the message field. We must include both the body string that we obtained through an ask for Action, and the attached files.

Clear the current variable (*Repeat Item*) in it. You can clear a variable by tapping on it and then selecting *Clear Variable* button in the panel. Or else, you can long press on it, and selecting *Clear Variable* in the popped-up menu.

Then tap on empty (*Message*) field, and select *Provided Input* from the *Select Variable* strip just above the onscreen keyboard. Let's rename it to *Body* for clarity. Dismiss the panel by tapping on X.

Tap on the *Body* variable, and you will see the same variable settings panel again. Tap on the button named *Return* so you are put inside the field. Make sure your blinking bar (cursor) is after the *Body* variable. Tap on the enter/return key on your keyboard to go to the next line. Now select *File* from among the magic variables. Rename it to *Attachments*.

That's all. The Shortcut is complete now. Test it. It works!

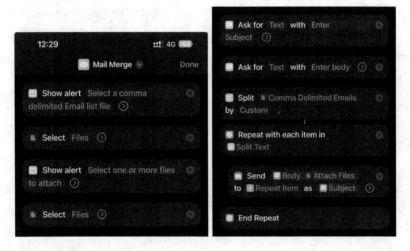

Automation

You have created a Shortcut, and now how are you going to run it? There are essentially two ways to execute a Shortcut.

1. Open the Shortcuts app and tap on the Shortcut to run it.

   Or you may run it by selecting **Share**, and then selecting the Shortcut name in the list. We learned how to enable a Shortcut in this Share panel.

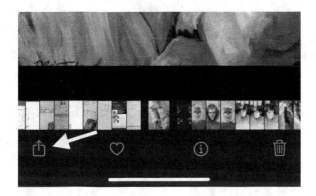

2. You can automate the Shortcut.

We are going to explore how you can automate Shortcuts in this chapter.

Automate means make something happens automatically (without your intervention) either periodically or in response to a particular trigger.

If something happens at a fixed time, for example, every hour, or 8.30 AM, it is periodic.

If something happens in response to something else (that "something else" is a trigger or event), it is event-driven or triggered.

So, you can make your Shortcuts run automatically at a fixed time or in response to some event. For that, we must open the *Automation* tab that you can find at the bottom middle of the

Shortcuts app. When you click on it, you will see something like the bottom right picture. In my device, I have not created any automation yet.

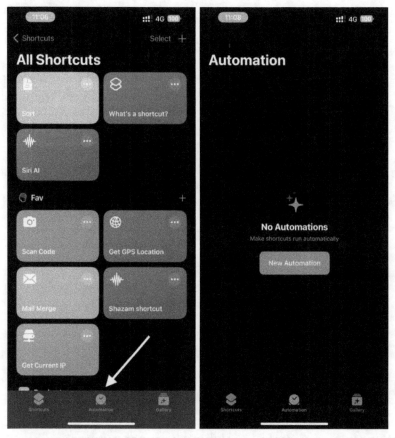

In Apple ecosystem, you have two kinds of automation – **Personal** and **Home**. It's Apple's own liking and nomenclature.

Home Automation

Home automation or office automation or any kind of automation for that matter is a distinct technical subject on its own; it's much involved and serious than Shortcuts. The main technology behind it is **IoT** (**Internet of Things**).

Apple, Google, and some other companies have introduced entire service lines catering to this segment (IoT and automation). Apple's version is known as *Home.* You can even find an app called **Home** on your Apple device.

With this (IoT and Home automation), you can do many marvelous things automated for you like:

It could automatically turn on or off lighting in your building at particular set times of the day, or as visitors enter in or leaves;

It could automatically open or close the window curtains or blinds at set times of the day or in response to the surrounding light intensity;

It could automatically turn on or off AC depending on the room temperature.

You could remotely monitor all of the electrical equipment operation, turn them on and off, control them, monitor the CCTV system, and so on.

The list is very long. Perhaps, I will write another book on this topic too.

Smart home or **smart office** is the common term. Actually, you can spend thousands of dollars to implement such a system; or if you are smart enough, you could achieve the same with much less money.

Therefore, we are not going to talk about Home automation in this book. You will learn about Personal automation only.

Personal Automation

So, what is personal automation? Simply put, it's making your Shortcuts automated. That is, a Shortcut will automatically run or trigger itself either at a particular set time, or in response to an event.

You will get what I just said with a very simple exercise. Let's do a simple example first.

Tap on *New Automation* button to create your first automation task. You will get a screen like below – the list is long, and therefore I have shown only two portions of the list.

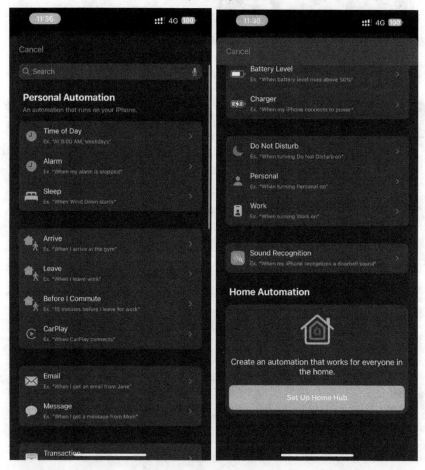

Read this screen well, and you can get some idea of what these options tell you. Let's read a few together.

Time of Day – if you select this option, it means that the Shortcut will automatically run at a particular time, like *At 8.00 AM, Weekdays*.

Arrive – If you take this option, your selected Shortcut will run when you (your device) arrive at a particular location (GPS needs to be turned on for this to work of course).

Email – The selected Shortcut will automatically trigger/run when you receive an email, for example, from a particular person. Or it may trigger when the received email has a specific word in its subject line.

Message – The selected Shortcut will automatically run when you receive an SMS from a particular person, for example.

Airplane Mode – This will run a Shortcut when you activate (or deactivate) the airplane mode of your device.

Wi-Fi – This will trigger your Shortcut when your device joins a particular WiFi network, for instance.

App – This will trigger the Shortcut when your selected app is opened (or closed).

Battery Level – A selected Shortcut will automatically run when the battery of the device falls below a set value.

NFC – It runs a Shortcut when a particular RF/NFC tag is tapped to the device.

Sound Recognition – It triggers when a specific (preset) sound is heard/sensed by the device.

As you can see now, it is not hard to get a good idea about what you can do with these triggers.

For our simple example, let's select *Time of Day* trigger/option. Tap on it.

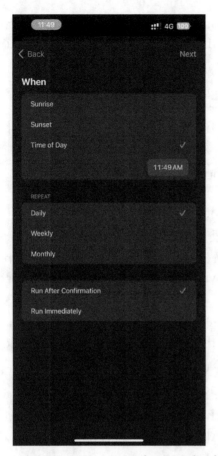

You got a new window with all the settings for that particular trigger. If you had selected a different trigger, this window will have entirely different set of settings. It's obvious. Right?

Let's explore a bit on this settings page. What exactly is the *sunrise time*? I don't know; maybe it's 6am.

Tap on *Sunrise*, you get a nice list of times relative to the sunrise. Fantastic!, Ok cancel the list.

Same goes with the *sunset*. You can set an absolute time with *Time of Day* too.

In the *Repeat* section, you can set how it should repeat – *daily*, *weekly*, or *monthly*. It's obvious for you to select what you want.

Anyway, click on each one of them. If you click on *Weekly*, you can see that you can individually select the days of week. Great! Go to Monthly option, and you can select which particular day of the month you want it to run on a monthly basis.

The last section lets you choose whether you want the selected Shortcut runs immediately without asking for your confirmation or not.

For our example, choose a particular time just a few minutes ahead of your current time with a daily basis (with or without asking for your confirmation).

At this moment, my time is 12:17PM, and therefore I set the trigger time to be *12:20PM*.

Then tap on *Next* to go to the next page.

Here, you have to select a Shortcut to run when this event occurs.

In my device, I have a few Shortcuts created by myself or installed from the Gallery, and I select one of them. I chose *Get GPS Location* Shortcut. Yours might be different. Select a Shortcut.

If you don't have any Shortcut in your device, please create one because you need a Shortcut to run. It's a must.

After I finished creating the automation, it is displayed like the bottom right image in the *Automation* tab.

Because it a Personal automation, it is listed under the heading *Personal*. It also gives you a summary (in this case, *At 12:20PM, daily Get GPS Location*).

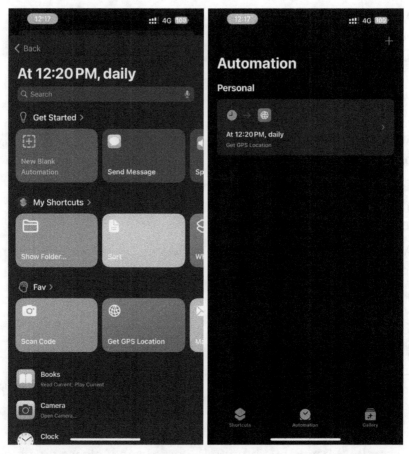

Now I am waiting earnestly until my Shortcut runs at the set time. It should work gracefully. Shouldn't it? It must work daily at 12:20PM.

It first asked for my confirmation with the following two pop-ups.

The first pop-up has a summary of the automation that is going to run.

I must tap on *Run* on the second pop-up to actually run it.

I confirmed by tapping on it, but still it failed. If an automation fails to run, it notifies you immediately with another pop-up. In my case, I got the following error.

An automation might fail due to a few reasons.

The Shortcut itself may not work because it has some errors in it. Then you must correct the Shortcut.

Some Shortcuts needs extra permissions and privileges to run. You should have enabled those permissions then.

For example, if the Shortcut is going to acquire your geographical position, the GPS must be enabled in your device first. In this case, I had disabled it. I think the automation should have worked perfectly if it had been enabled. Let's check it.

We can't wait until 12.20PM in the next day to see the new result after I enabled the GPS in my device. Can we? So, let's either modify the automation or delete it and create a new one.

You can delete the previous personal automation very easily by swiping left on the automation (bottom left picture) and tapping on the <u>red</u> *Delete* button (bottom right picture).

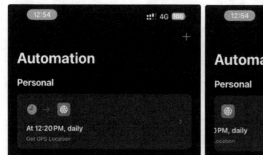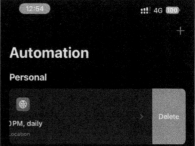

I am going to modify the automation without deleting it. Just tap on the automation to go into the automation editor window.

Tap on each field and you can intuitively understand what they are. You can modify to include a different Shortcut, modify the trigger times, and modify whether you need to confirm.

This time I will change to *Run Immediately* and toggle on the *Notify When Run* option so I will not get a notification that the device is going to run an automation. I changed the time a few minutes ahead of my current time again.

I enabled the GPS sensor (ie, Location Services) in my device settings too.

It worked nicely this time.

Send SMS When Somebody Emails You

Let's create a new automation that will send you an SMS when you receive an email from a specific person.

First, you must create a Shortcut to message you (via SMS). Go to the *Shortcuts* tab of your Shortcuts app. Create a new Shortcut named `Message Me`.

Insert a *Send Message* Action. In the *recipient* field, enter the recipient's mobile number, and a meaningful string in the *message* field.

That's it for the Shortcut. Then go to the *Automation* tab. Tap on + at the top right corner, and you'll get the familiar list of triggers.

This automation is triggered on (receiving of) email. So, select Email trigger. It takes you the properties panel of that trigger. You have many options here. Carefully study them.

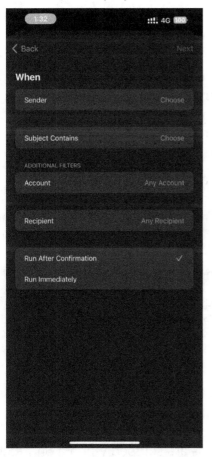

This trigger can get activated on several criteria – the sender email, the recipient email, what is inside the subject line of the email.

In our example, we want to trigger it when an email comes from *sumith@tekcroach.top*. Therefore, I tap on *Choose* field in front of the Sender, and enter `sumith@tekcroach.top`. I also set it to *Run Immediately*. In your example, change the email accordingly (don't input my email address).

Then, I tap on *Next* to select the *Message Me* Shortcut we created a moment ago.

Test it now. Send an email from that email address to any email address you have added in your **Mail** app.

Commenting

Comment is an essential thing in programming; actually, we are using it in our day-to-day life in its many disguised forms like documentation, manual, catalog, etc. All of these give us details about something – be it a machine, an electrical appliance, a computer program, a Shortcut, or an Action.

In Shortcuts, commenting is mainly intended for Shortcut creators like you and me. We sometimes create complicated Shortcuts, or we employ Actions to do tricks. But we would not remember the intricacies of the Shortcut after some time. You can write "short notes" (ie, comments) near such Actions inside the Shortcut itself to remind you the necessary details of it.

Let's modify the above Shortcut to include a few comments at necessary points. Open the *Mail Merge* Shortcut.

Say you want to include a comment at the very top of the Shortcut.

Comment is available as an Action (almost everything is available as Actions in Shortcuts). *Comment* Action does nothing. It just lets you create a comment. A comment never gets executed. *Comment* Actions are skipped when a Shortcut runs. Comment is intended to show up only in the Shortcut editor screen.

Add a *Comment* Action now. Drag it to the very top.

Comment Actions are shown in a different color for you to identify them easily.

Write something as the comment. I intend to use this topmost (first) comment to introduce the Shortcut. So, I would write something like "`This Shortcut lets you select one or several files to be attached to an email, and it will get the recipient email addresses from a CSV file (email addresses separated by a comma).`"

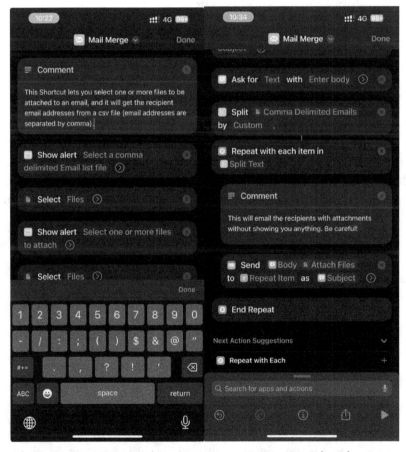

Always write a very descriptive comment, or else the comment will be useless. If you wrote very cryptic short comments, the reader would not understand the comment itself and would not be able to relate the comment to the Shortcut.

Let's add another comment to describe what the *Send email* Action is going to do. Therefore, we must position this comment just above *Send email* action. Drag it there and write something like "`This will email the recipients with attachments without showing you anything. Be careful!`" (See above right image).

Shortcuts for MAC

Shortcuts work across all the Apple products – iPhones, iPads, MAC computers, and Apple watches.

However, every kind of device may not support all the Actions. There are some Actions only applicable to MAC; some Actions cannot be run on Apple Watch, for example.

So far, we have been running Shortcuts on either iPhone or iPad. Now let's see how your Shortcuts are run on MAC computers in brief.

Note that not all versions of MAC operating system support Shortcuts. Only newer versions support it. In case your MAC computer has an older operating system, you must upgrade the OS.

> As we all know, Apple has the disgusting (mostly bloody marketing) practice of discontinuing OS upgrades after a few years, and you will be stuck with an old MAC OS forever.

> Will you? "apple-officially" Yes!, But practically you can easily hack the system with free and easy tools like **OpenCore Patcher** that will allow you to upgrade the OS to the newest. Don't worry about so-called security concerns, and upgrade your old MacOS now.

If you use the same Apple ID in both your mobile device and in the MAC, and if you have enabled iCloud for Shortcuts, then the Shortcuts you create on your mobile device are automatically made available in your Mac. In fact, they will be available in all the devices logged in using the same Apple ID, for that matter.

How to enable iCloud for Shortcuts in your mobile device? Open the *Settings* app on your iPhone.

Tap the topmost setting which is about your Apple ID, iCloud, Media & Purchases.

Tap *iCloud.* Tap *Show All.*

Toggle on the *Shortcuts.* That's all.

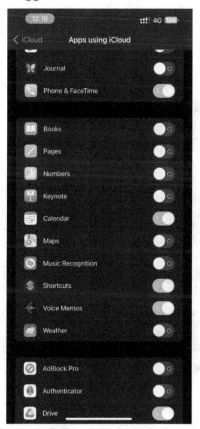

You must do the same on your MAC. Click on the Apple symbol at the leftmost end of the menu bar.

Click on *System Settings…* A dialog box appears.

Click on the topmost setting which is about Apple ID, in the left navigation bar of the dialog box.

Click on *iCloud* setting in the right settings page of the dialog box.

Click on *Show More Apps…* in the right settings page.

Toggle on the *Shortcuts* setting in the new settings box. Click on *Done*, and close the dialog box. That's all.

Now open the Shortcuts app on your MAC to see the Shortcuts installed on your MAC. You can open it from either the **Applications** folder or the **Launchpad** easily.

If you possibly do not see the *Shortcuts* app on your MAC, you probably have an older MacOS installed. You can and should upgrade (officially or unofficially) the MacOS as I have mentioned a few paragraphs back.

Not only can it automatically import the Shortcuts stored in your other device, you can also create new Shortcuts in this app. Only the user interface is a bit different. You can become familiar with the new interface within a few minutes. No learning curve at all!

To create a new Shortcut, click on the + sign at the top middle of the app. You will get a new Shortcut creation window.

You can rename the Shortcut by clicking on *Title* at the top. You see all the Actions in the right pane of the window. If you can't see the Actions, click on the 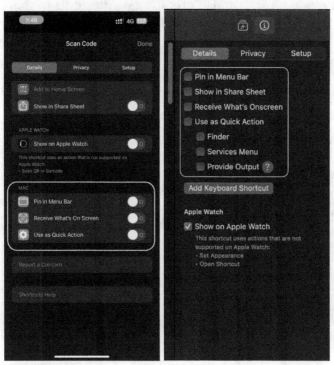 symbol at the top bar of the window. Hover on that symbol and you will see a tooltip of *Action Library*.

You can find Actions just as you do in the mobile device. Then double click on the Action or drag it onto the middle Shortcut creation pane. Nothing new here!

You can rename, edit, or delete Shortcuts by right clicking on Shortcut tiles.

The Shortcuts you create on the MAC are automatically shown in the mobile device too if the both devices are using the same iCloud account.

There are a few options specifically designed for MAC. Look in the *Details* screen of a Shortcut in the mobile device's Shortcuts app to see these three options – *Pin in Menu Bar, Receive What's On Screen,* and *Use as Quick Action.*

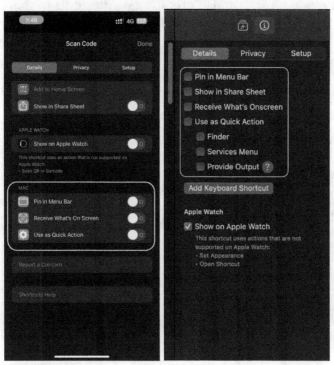

You can get the same settings page on the MAC by clicking on the ⓘ symbol on the top bar in the Shortcut creation screen. I have shown in the above right image the relevant part of the screen for you to compare the both side by side.

Pin in Menu Bar obviously means your Shortcut will be shown in the **Menu Bar** of MacOS. Here, my MAC has one Shortcut named *Get Current IP* pinned onto the Menu.

Having Shortcuts on the Menu Bar makes it easier for you to directly run a Shortcut without going through the hassle of opening the Shortcuts app.

If you click on the little curved arrow head in front of the Shortcut name, you are directly taken to the Shortcut editor, and you can edit that Shortcut.

Use as Quick Action makes your Shortcut available under **Quick Actions** menu. You can access the Quick Actions menu by right clicking on any file or folder on the MAC.

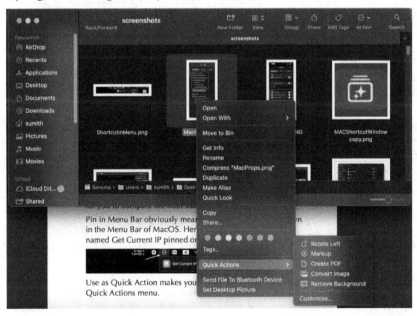

Finalization

We are going to end our journey soon. In this chapter, we will be touching on miscellaneous things.

Every Shortcut has a name, an icon, and even a color. You can change them all.

On your mobile device, open the Shortcuts app and open the Shortcut editor screen (either by tapping on ... on the particular Shortcut tile or long-pressing on the tile and selecting *Edit* in the menu). Then tap on the Shortcut icon beside the Shortcut name at the top of the screen. Select a color and/or an icon. That's it.

You can change the icon and the color from within the MAC version of the Shortcuts app too. Right-click on the particular Shortcut tile, and select *Change Icon...* Then change the color and/or the icon.

You can share a Shortcut on your device (MAC or mobile) just like you share any other file.

On the mobile device, open the Shortcuts app, long-press on a Shortcut tile, select *Share* from the pop-up menu, and the rest is up to you.

From this Share option, you can add a Shortcut to your Home Screen too.

Automating Personal Hotspot

When you create a personal automation, I told you that you must already have a Shortcut to select. Well, that is a half-truth. After you have chosen the preferred trigger/event, you tap on *Next*. Then you have the option not to select an already existing Shortcut and instead you tap on *New Blank Automation*. You are taken to a window where you can create a brand new Shortcut.

Let's create an automation to practice this. Create a new automation.

Select the *Leave* as the trigger. It will trigger when you leave a particular location (ie, your home, or gym, or any place for that matter).

Populate the *Location* field. I selected my Home location, for example. I set it to *Run Immediately* and *Any Time* options.

If you like, you could specify a time range within when this automation must be activated. Even if you leave that chosen place, the automation won't still trigger if you leave outside this set period.

Tap on *Next*, and choose *New Blank Automation*.

Create your Shortcut there. You know the rest now.

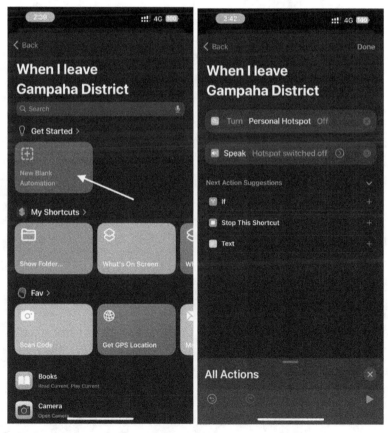

As the Shortcut, I included two Actions – *Set Personal Hotspot*, and *Speak Text*.

The *Set Personal Hotspot* Action is shown in a different name after it is added; the shown name is like *Turn Personal Hotspot On*. If you tap on *On* (or *Off*), it will toggle to *Off* (or *On*). In the same way, tap on *Turn*, and you will see another new option *Toggle* there.

What is the difference between *Turn* (on/off) and *Toggle?* *Turn* is absolute while *Toggle* is relative. *Turn on* always turns on and *Turn off* always turns off. However, *Toggle* turns on if it is already off or turns off if it is already on.

Write something like `Hotspot Switched off` in the *Speak Text* Action so it will read it aloud when this automation gets activated.

Now on, when you leave the set place, the personal hotspot will be automatically switched off. That's a good thing to do. You should implement its complementary automation as well; that is to automatically re-activate the personal hotspot when you arrive at a particular place.

Create a new automation. Use the *Arrive* trigger for that. Include the same *Set Personal Hotspot* Action with its field set to *On*. Optionally you could include a *Speak Text* Action with a text like `Hotspot switched on`.

Shortcut Inside a Shortcut

You can run another Shortcut from within a Shortcut. With this feature, it is possible to kind of merge several Shortcuts to achieve a complex task.

Create a Shortcut as usual. Then at the required moment, run another existing Shortcut. Then insert more Actions, if any. Likewise, you can run one or several Shortcuts at different points of your Shortcut.

To run a Shortcut, we must use the *Run Shortcut* Action.

To practice it, we'll run two Shortcuts we created earlier from within our new Shortcut.

Create a new Shortcut named `SuperShortcut`.

Insert a *Show Alert* with the text "`We are going to run two Shortcuts`".

Insert a *Run Shortcut* Action. Tap on its Shortcut field and select *Get GPS Location* we created earlier (or some other Shortcut).

Then insert a *Show Alert* again with the text "`One is still pending`".

Add another *Run Shortcut* Action. This time, choose *Get Current IP* (or some other) Shortcut.

Insert another *Show Alert* with the text "`Thanks`"

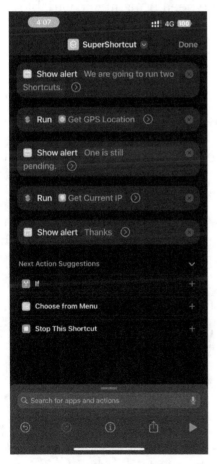

If you remember, both the *Get GPS Location* and the *Get Current IP* Shortcuts copy its output to the clipboard. So, in this

131

Shortcut, the *Get GPS Location* is run first and its output is copied to the clipboard. Then, it runs the *Get Current IP* which again saves its output in the clipboard. Now, what was previously stored in the clipboard is overwritten.

If you want to keep the both outputs in the clipboard without modifying the original two Shortcuts, you can achieve it in several ways.

User-defined Variables

For the first time in our journey, we are going to create and use user-defined variables. We have been using magic variables so far.

You know a variable is a named memory location where you can save something temporarily, and then you can access it using the variable name.

My thinking is like this. After running the first internal Shortcut, I will save the content of the Clipboard to a variable. Then I know I can retrieve that content now stored in the variable later in my Shortcut. After that, I don't care if the clipboard is overwritten or not. I have an exact copy of the clipboard.

Likewise, I will create another variable after the second internal Shortcut; actually, this is redundant because the clipboard is not overwritten this time, but let's go ahead to practice with variables.

In this example, I show the both outputs on screen in the end.

To create a variable, we must use *Set Variable* Action. It has two compulsory fields to be filled in by us.

The first field is the variable name. Type in a short descriptive name. In the first case, I typed Loc because I am going to store the location details in it.

The second field (*input* after *to*) is the source. Tap on it and you will see all the variables that you can select. Select *Clipboard* from the list because we want to copy the clipboard.

Duplicate the *Set Variable* Action and change its variable name to IP. That's all.

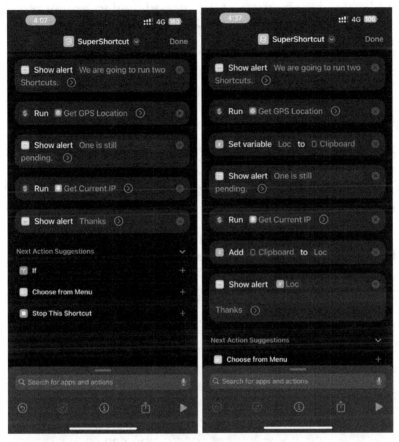

You can create as many variables as you want. But you can keep adding (appending) data to an existing variable, if you like. It may be neat and tidy.

We must use *Add to Variable* Action to "reuse" the same variable. It too has two mandatory fields to be filled in.

The first field *Input* must be the data/content you want to append.

The second field *Variable Name* is the variable name to which the data is appended. If there is already no variable with that name, a new variable is created.

So, let's modify our previous Shortcut. Delete the second *Set Variable* Action and Insert *Add to Variable* Action there. Set its input field to *Clipboard,* and the second field to Loc (write Loc). Modify the last *Show Alert* Action to only include *Loc* variable (delete the non-existing *IP* variable). The Shortcut should look like the above right image.

An automation for "Squirmers"

We all go to the bed with our iPhone, I know. When we turn to sides or "squirm" in bed, the phone screen automatically rotates. It is sometimes annoying with some apps (especially I don't like it happening when I am using Telegram).

You could lock the **orientation** manually. But we can automate it. In this example, I am going to lock the orientation when I am opening Telegram, and unlock it when I am closing it.

Create a new automation. Select the *App* trigger.

In the coming page, select *Is Opened* (by default it is selected). Set Run Immediately. Select *Telegram* (or whatever app you want) in the *App* field.

Tap on *Next.* Select *New Blank Automation.*

Insert *Set Orientation Lock* Action. It will be shown as *Toggle orientation lock.* If you tap on *Toggle,* you can see its other options. But leave it like that for now. That's it.

Now when I rotate the phone, the Telegram app does not change its orientation because it has locked the screen orientation. Fantastic!

But even if I close/leave the app, still the orientation lock is active. I do not want that.

Run Telegram (or your chosen app) again, and now the orientation lock is gone! That's not what we wanted again. The culprit is the *Toggle* in the Set Orientation Lock Action. Change it to *Turn* ... on. That problem solved!

Let's solve the first problem now. I want to unlock it when I close or leave the app. Therefore, we must add another automation to toggle the orientation automatically when I close or leave Telegram. Now you can do that too. Right? Perfect!

Finally...

Explore the Actions. Play with them. Study many Shortcuts in the Gallery with the new knowledge you've acquired through this book.

Some Actions are provided by apps installed on your device. For example, you will have such Actions as *Send Message Via WhatsApp, Send Photo via WhatsApp* if you have installed WhatsApp.

I hope you will create your own Shortcuts to make your life more productive, easier, and fun. Good Luck!

www.ingramcontent.com/pod-product-compliance
Lightning Source LLC
LaVergne TN
LVHW051655050326
832903LV00032B/3826